PRAISE FOR *WHAT BELIEF CAN DO*

"Ron Archer's story is captivating. As a 'trick baby,' his life was miraculously spared, and there's no question in my mind it was for God's Kingdom purpose. Ron is one of the most gifted communicators I know. I believe with his eyes fixed on Jesus and with a love for God and all his neighbors, he can help lead the too-often overlooked and 'least of these' into a Promised Land life. He has supernaturally been transformed by the power of the Gospel, and he wants everyone to experience the divine encounter Jesus referred to as being 'born from above.' I don't think you'll be able to put this book down, and everyone who cares about the future of freedom will want to hear him share not only his heart, but the heart of his heavenly Father."

JAMES ROBISON
Founder and president, LIFE Outreach International
Fort Worth, Texas

"For the past few years, I have been tremendously blessed by the ministry and friendship of Ron Archer. In his new book *What Belief Can Do*, he shares his own horrific life experiences with a transparency and humility that will grip your heart and revive your spirit with a fresh impartation of hope and inspiration. This book will literally be a game changer for everyone who reads it. In this literary work, Ron demonstrates the possibilities, growth, and potential that can be accessed when we tap into the power that lies at the core of what we believe. Read this book and experience the power!"

JENNIFER R. BIARD
Senior pastor, Jackson Revival Center Church
Jackson, Mississippi

"Dr. Ron Archer is a dynamic communicator, servant leader, passionate entrepreneur, and global icon. Dr. Archer's transformational life story will fill you with incredible hope and inspire you to believe in God for what seems impossible. It is a game changer."

LARRY KAUFMAN
Lead pastor, Grace Mennonite Church
Berlin, Ohio

"Ron and I met thirty-seven years ago as college freshmen at Baldwin Wallace College (now University). Ron was very much engaged in campus ministry, teaching Bible studies and leading prayer meetings, as well as being involved in Fellowship of Christian Athletes (where Ron arranged for me to give my first public testimony).

"I entered Ron's world early into his budding ministry on campus and at Good Shepherd Baptist Church. It was Ron's involvement, witness, teaching, and preaching that became the catalyst for my coming to faith in Christ and subsequent call to ministry at Baldwin Wallace. I quickly became an extension to campus evangelism and started driving carloads of students across town on Sunday mornings to Good Shepherd Baptist Church in Ron's old station wagon (with the floor rusted out on the driver's side).

"I read Ron's new book, intending to skim each chapter to get the essence of the story I thought I knew after thirty-seven years of friendship, but I found myself drawn into an unfolding journey toward Christ—filled with trauma, drama, powerful overcoming, and rising to levels of greatness—that I could readily identify with from my own journey toward and in Christ. It is a must-read for all, especially those who find themselves in the throes of life and needing the inspiration to rise above present circumstances and discover and actualize God's purpose for their lives."

BISHOP JOSEPH WILSON
CEO and president, Power 2 Become Ministries, Inc.

"Miracles happen when we believe. Ron Archer is a living testimony that the circumstances of birth do not define us when we believe. The paths that the world draws us into are seductive and easy, unless we believe. *What Belief Can Do* is Ron Archer's journey from destruction to destiny; from crushing racial oppression to worldwide influencer; from child of the gutter to man of God. Ron Archer is a walking miracle of God, and this book reveals how God is always at work to bring that same miracle into all of our lives. Get it, read it, and believe!"

JOR-EL GODSEY
President, Heartbeat International

"A roller coaster of emotions and injections of reality all in one life as God orchestrates it. An account that extinguishes excuses for failure like putting a fire hose to a single matchstick. An account that screams purpose, perseverance, and passion from start to finish."

ERIC PETERS
Senior pastor, Power in the Blood Assembly, Barbados;
International field representative, Samaritan's Purse

"A story of redemption which has inspired and brought new hope into my life. Reading it was like going from the valley of the shadow of death to places of resting water and green pastures. I am so proud to have met Dr. Ronaldo Archer; it fills my eyes with tears and my heart with deep gratitude. I am also grateful to have met Skeezix, his heroic mother, his intrepid aunt, and his sister. Thanks so much for this amazing book."

RANDY GUILLÉN
Pastor and business consultant,
son of God, husband, father of seven kids

WHAT BELIEF CAN DO

RON ARCHER
WITH MIKE YORKEY

WHAT BELIEF CAN DO

HOW GOD TURNED MY PAIN INTO POWER AND TRAGEDY
INTO TRIUMPH—AND HOW HE CAN DO THE SAME FOR YOU

SALEM
BOOKS
an imprint of Regnery Publishing

CONTENTS

PROLOGUE

My mother didn't know how to hide a gun very well.

Maybe she thought her ten-year-old son wouldn't go snooping around the master bedroom and find the snub-nosed revolver in her nightstand. Maybe she thought it was more important to keep a gun nearby in case Dick Archer, her estranged and abusive husband, came back to the house bent on hurting or even killing her. Whatever the case, I knew Mom had a gun, and I knew where to find it.

And I had a mind to use it, too. Even though Dick Archer was no longer around to beat me or my mother, life was far from easy at home. Mom was doing all she could to keep it all together, struggling to put food on the table as best as she knew how, but she often took her frustrations out on me. There were moments when Mom thrashed me pretty good if I did something to tick her off, so I became the quietest kid you could imagine. Whatever Mom wanted or demanded of me, I did so without complaint. I didn't want to get another spanking or tongue-lashing for doing something wrong.

And then there was the all-black elementary school I attended in our urban neighborhood close to downtown Cleveland, Ohio. At one time, I had loved school, but now I dreaded taking a seat in my classroom because I stuttered like Porky Pig.

My incessant stuttering and inability to finish a sentence opened the door to unmerciful teasing by other kids. I was in the schoolyard for recess one morning when my classmates decided to play "Ring around the Rosie." Suddenly, I found myself sur-rounded by a half-dozen kids. They encircled me and started a chant they had obviously practiced:

His name is Renardo, he is a retardo.
He sits on the steeple and spits at the people.

That nursery rhyme made the rounds at my elementary school. I heard it repeated many times in the schoolyard. There was noth-ing I could do except swallow the indignation as best I could.

Ignored, berated, or beaten at home and teased at school, I had really had enough. Nobody knew how desperate and alone and scared and miserable and hopeless I felt. All I could think was *If the next ten years are anything like the last ten years, then I don't want any more years.*

I was supposed to dream of becoming a Cleveland Browns running back like Jim Brown, or of becoming a fireman or a police-man, or maybe of blasting off into space as an astronaut someday.

But I didn't have any of those dreams. I didn't have *any* dreams, and that's why there was nothing to live for.

At this, my lowest point, I had no vision of who I could become or what I might achieve. I had no inkling that pain wasn't the end of my story, that one day God would redeem the mess of my life, and that my story would inspire millions in their own struggles. I did not know God, and I had no concept of the tremendous power of belief—of belief in myself and, more important, of belief in God. I had no idea what that belief could do. All that would come later.

In that moment, all I felt was my pain.

I held the gun in my right hand and raised it to my head. I pressed the barrel against my temple.

Without any hesitation, I pulled the trigger.

PART 1

TOUGH TIMES

1
—

LIFE WITH GRANNIE

I thought all grandmothers were white.

I had an incredibly close bond with Grannie, who was white as a marble statue. Born Greta Strasse, she was the daughter of German immigrants, yet she chose to marry a coal-black Cuban immigrant in the 1940s, a time when interracial marriage was as rare as a passing comet.

Greta and Tony Peru met while World War II was gripping the country. One time after his factory shift, Tony walked into a Woolworth's in downtown Cleveland. Known as a five-and-dime store, every Woolworth's featured a lunch counter where meals were served on the cheap. Tuna sandwiches and hot dogs were a dime; coffee and soda were a nickel.

Tony slid onto a red leatherette-covered stool at the lunch counter, where a friendly waitress took his order.

I don't know who flirted first. I don't know when their eyes locked and they made a connection. I don't know how many times

Tony visited Woolworth's before he got the courage to ask Greta to meet him in a park or a restaurant in the black neighborhood of Cleveland—because he certainly couldn't meet her in her world. All I know is that sometime in 1943, she said yes to meeting him in secret.

Tony told her his story. He had traveled from Cuba to the Gulf Coast of Alabama by boat ten years earlier when he was sixteen years old. After stepping on American soil, he took any job he could get as a day laborer, working a hoe in cotton fields as far as the eye could see or picking peaches and pecans at harvesttime. He made fifty cents a day toiling from sunup to sundown and bunking in lean-to shacks, where he slept on hay and straw and wore the same clothes for weeks at a time without any washing. He was fed scraps from the farmer's table and sometimes had to eat what the goats were given—Whalf-eaten cobs of corn. That's what he did to survive.

He had to learn English. But he also had to be a quick study and be quiet about it because if he was too bold, too mouthy, or too independent, he would be considered "uppity" and need a reminder of who was really in charge in the Deep South—the white establishment. He witnessed foremen beating farm workers for the slightest infraction, saw bound black men hanging from tree limbs following a lynching, and came upon white crosses burning brightly in the night.

The United States' entry into World War II after Pearl Harbor changed everything for Tony. As mobilization transformed an idle economy into a powerhouse economic engine, there was an unprecedented military production of arms and ammunition: hundreds of ships; tens of thousands of aircraft, tanks, cannons, and jeeps; and millions of rifles and bullets. This resulted in a huge demand for labor in the nation's factories, mainly concentrated in the steel-producing cities of Pennsylvania and Ohio. Tony heard that blacks were being hired for the first time to work in those factories.

He hitchhiked—and walked—over seven hundred miles from Birmingham to Cleveland, dreaming of a better life.

Greta, four years younger than Tony, never told her parents she was seeing a black man. She couldn't. She knew that. Her parents were from the Old Country. In their eyes, there was just no way a black man and a white woman could be romantically involved. Yet Tony and Greta got married anyway and started a family.

Their first child, Elizabeth—my mother—was born on June 11, 1945, and was followed by six more children: Michael, Kelly, David, Carl, Antoinette, and Anita. Most of the Peru children, with their straight hair and fair skin, could pass for white even though their father was black like his African ancestors who had reached Cuba on slave ships.

In the late 1950s, my grandparents were walking arm in arm on a Cleveland sidewalk when a white man stopped my grandmother and asked her why she was with a big, ugly guy like my grandfather. Actually, the white man used the N word, which lit a fuse. My grandfather reared back, swung his clenched fist, and broke the man's neck. A jury sentenced him to ten years in state prison for socking a white man. The family lost their house in Buckeye, a Cleveland suburb, and moved to Hough, a gritty neighborhood close to downtown. My grandmother found a two-story house with two units—one up, one down—and took the second floor. She cleaned homes to keep a roof over her family's heads and food on the table.

Most of the time all my grandmother could afford was a gunnysack of russet potatoes—and that was when they were on sale. The menu was always the same: potato pancakes for breakfast, a watery potato soup for lunch, and potato slices browned in shortening for dinner.

Michael, a year younger than my mother, and his younger brothers, David and Carl, became food scavengers. They'd bring home fresh loaves of bread that "fell off" a Wonder Bread truck or fruits and vegetables they had stuffed into their pockets when the local grocer wasn't looking.

That's how they lived.

That's how they survived.

•   •   •

Grannie was respected in our predominantly black neighborhood. She was shown courtesy and given a wide berth because she was a white woman who chose to live in the ghetto, raising a large family and doing the best she could with what she had. Black men tipped their hats, and black women included her in the neighborhood gossip.

And then I came along on June 15, 1963. If you do the math, Mom had just turned seventeen years old four days earlier. I was born four weeks premature and weighed four pounds, two ounces. My lungs were underdeveloped, which impacted my breathing. I battled pneumonia right off the bat. I was a sickly child, always struggling with pneumonia and earaches.

A couple of months after my arrival, my unmarried mother moved to New York City to make money, leaving me in Grannie's care. I wouldn't see Mom for nearly two years. During that time, my grandmother was an incredible nurturing presence— feeding me, changing me, bathing me, and rocking me in her fleshy arms when I cried out to be comforted. She cheered my first steps and helped me form my first words.

She had plenty of Old World experience to draw upon. Once I was crying uncontrollably when it was time to change my diaper, but Grannie had a solution. She put a towel down on the dining room table and then laid me on top. Before she started changing me, she reached up and gave the chandelier a gentle push. The rocking motion of the chandelier silenced me. I was mesmerized by the dazzling swaying of the shimmering glass beads above me.

Grannie's upstairs unit had a rat problem. These Norway rats would come crawling out of the toilet in the middle of the night, sniffing for food. If they caught the scent of milk on your breath, the rats would chew off your lips or part of your nose. At least that's what Grannie had read in the newspaper, so she was on high alert and wasn't going to take any chances, especially with a baby in the house. She and my aunts took steak knives with them every time they went into the bathroom. It was my uncles, though, who eventually "solved" the rat issue. They put a cinder block on top of the toilet seat cover after it got dark so the rats couldn't get out.

Life with Grannie wasn't always so eventful. She loved me and found a way to take care of me, day in and day out, even though she was on her own and raising my aunts and uncles, too. I was too young at the time to know or care why Grannie bore so many burdens by herself. But years after I had lived with her, Grannie told me why we never saw her parents, the Strasses. Talking about them was enough to get the tears flowing.

"Oh, Skeezix," she moaned, using the nickname she gave me. "They didn't want to see me after I got married. They even had a funeral for me and filled a small casket with my clothes, scrapbooks, pictures, and high school diploma. They said I was dead to them."

As a result, Grannie felt isolated and alone. She was abandoned by the Strasses for marrying my grandfather, but it was worse than that. With her husband in prison, their marriage was practically over. Even after my grandfather was released, he and Grannie did not reunite as husband and wife. I never learned the details of what happened—it just wasn't talked about. All I knew was that he and Grannie would live separately for the rest of their lives, showing up together only at large family gatherings held on the Fourth of July, Labor Day, Thanksgiving, or Christmas. In fact, those were some of the only times I saw Big Daddy—as I called my grandfather—when I was growing up.

Despite the care Grannie showed her family, she was a sorrowful, despondent woman. She had lost her husband, her house, and her good job. She had ridden a chute from the middle class to poverty. When you consider that her family disowned her because she married a black man, it was no great surprise that Grannie was depressed much of the time. Most days it seemed like only I could put a smile on her face.

Her disfigured face.

A year or two before I was born, Grannie experienced fainting spells. She was cleaning homes to feed seven hungry kids and put a roof over their heads, so she was under enormous pressure. Grannie was cleaning a bathroom one day when she suddenly felt lightheaded and had to sit down for a minute. On another occasion, she told me that her world turned black when she was behind the wheel. Grannie averted an accident, but that incident told her that something was seriously wrong.

She made an appointment with her family physician, who referred her to a specialist. The specialist ran several tests, and a few weeks later, Grannie learned some very bad news: she had a cancerous tumor in her brain just behind the left eye.

Back then, cancer treatment was fairly crude compared to today: a neurosurgeon would do his best to cut the malignant mass out of the body while the family hoped he got it all. For my grandmother, the news got worse: during the procedure, her surgeon had to remove her left eye as well as parts of her skull and a small fragment of the frontal lobe of the brain to save her life.

She survived the operation, but my mother, aunts, and uncles claimed she was never the same. They said the gruesome procedure changed her personality drastically. She was no longer outgoing, no longer adventurous, and no longer active. Bedeviled by depression, mood swings, and headaches, she became quiet and shy. She felt deformed and ashamed. Grannie believed that people thought she was ugly.

Her glass eye never looked right to me, but the artificial eye was hidden behind humongous tinted glasses she wore every waking minute, day or night, indoors or outdoors, sun or no sun. It was the only thing she could do to hide the glass eye and the botched job the surgeon did while sewing her up.

I didn't know Grannie before the operation, so I never saw her outgoing, adventurous side. But I loved her all the same, and she clearly loved me.

Despite all that she had endured, Grannie took care of her family the best she could. Grannie was a survivor. And in many ways, I would become one as well.

2

THE ARCHER HOME

When my mother returned from New York City, she met a black man named Dick Archer at a nightclub, and he immediately began to court her. He was in his early thirties, a dozen years older than Mom, and a college graduate making a good life for himself by managing real estate properties for a growing clientele. Dick showed that he was a good guy by bringing a sack of groceries and jars of Gerber baby food whenever he dropped by my grandmother's place to call on Mom. Because of my mother's stunning beauty, he viewed her as a potential trophy wife on his arm, but something about Elizabeth intrigued him beyond her gorgeous looks. Dick really liked my mother's spunk and believed she had the potential to do anything she wanted in life.

One of the popular Broadway plays at the time was *My Fair Lady*, a musical about a London professor named Henry Higgins who takes an interest in Eliza Doolittle, a Cockney flower peddler. Professor Higgins has studied phonetics, and believes that if he can teach Eliza to speak properly, he can turn her into a lady of respectable social standing.

Dick saw himself as Professor Higgins and my mother as his Eliza Doolittle. He would transform this young filly who didn't want to be controlled by anyone, including someone clamoring to be a father figure in her life, into a cultured, mature woman and adoring wife. My mother initially rebuffed his romantic efforts, but as he laid on his charm, showing up at Grannie's doorstep with flowers and treating her like a lady, my mother's attitude slowly came around.

"Let's settle down," he said. "I will take care of you."

And that's all it took for this Eliza Doolittle to say yes to Professor Higgins. For someone who had lived in such precarious circumstances as my mother, a stable life was too great a prospect to ignore.

My mother was hesitant to marry him, however, which I didn't learn until years later. In the meantime, I remember very distinctly hearing my mother say that Dick Archer was my father. At such a young age I accepted and internalized that declaration, but I thought it odd that he wasn't very hands-on with me. I thought fathers were supposed to be friendly and play catch with their sons, like I saw other kids doing in the neighborhood with their fathers, but Dad—as I called him—never seemed interested in what I was doing. I have no memories of him teaching me how to swing a bat, shoot a basketball, or catch a long pass. He never walked me to the nearby convenience store to buy me an ice cream on Sunday afternoons.

We lived in a brownstone apartment that Dad was managing. Our two-bedroom place wasn't far from Grannie, which helped ease the transition for me. We still saw Grannie a lot, especially after my sister, Crystal, was born shortly before I turned three years old. At that age, I didn't understand what was happening around me and preferred to play outside with my best friend B. D. in the sandy dirt surrounding our eight-unit apartment complex, which was filled with black single moms who had two, three, or four children underfoot. There was no grass and no greenery, but B. D. and I had fun rolling our toy trucks and jabbing our sticks into ant holes.

One childhood memory I've never forgotten relates to my father's massive dog—a gnarly German shepherd that he used to protect the property at night. The dog's name was Death, which seemed appropriate given how aggressive he was. I loved him just the same. He was as big as a Shetland pony but could turn vicious in a second if he felt threatened or needed to protect us. Death was the most-feared dog in the neighborhood.

One time I learned just how protective he could be. Late one afternoon, I dropped a banana into his food dish—and then realized I had forgotten to peel it. When I reached into his bowl, Death thought I was trying to take his food. He bit me so hard on the nose that he crunched cartilage and broke bone. I wailed in great pain for hours—and didn't get near his food dish again. Not long after that incident, they got rid of the dog.

When I started kindergarten at Gracemount Elementary School— an inner-city school known as "The Mount"—I heard my teacher say "Ronaldo Archer" during roll call. This cemented in my mind that Dick Archer really was my father.

I liked kindergarten because I loved my teacher, Mrs. Jones, who was an older white woman. Where my black classmates saw a white teacher, I saw a relative. I felt a similar affinity for her as I did for Grannie. I didn't fear white people as some of my black friends did. Instead, I listened closely to her instructions, and I showed her that I liked learning, recess, and nap time.

The highlight of my year was when Mrs. Jones asked me to play the lead role in the Christmas production of *The Little Drummer Boy*. This was the first time I ever felt special—like I was singled out. Walking onstage with my drum, I basked in the applause and loved the attention.

That same year we moved into a two-story brick Tudor home on Stockbridge Avenue in the Lee-Harvard neighborhood, which was also predominantly black. It was 1968, and Cleveland was on edge following the assassination of Martin Luther King Jr.

Several of my uncles—teens at the time—had rampaged on the streets and participated in the looting and arson following King's assassination. One of them put the muzzle of a shotgun in a man's mouth and robbed him. My uncle didn't pull the trigger, but he was sent to state prison for attempted murder. I remember visiting him not long afterward and my mother and grandmother telling me on the drive that he was in the military. I had no reason to doubt what they said, and I certainly thought so when I spotted him and the other prisoners wearing similar uniforms of blue shirts and blue jeans. The noise was extremely loud, and my mother and grandmother cried because of the numbing reality they witnessed.

• • •

I loved school, but my early school years were marked by illness. I was always sick because my ears, nose, and throat didn't work properly. I'd go from an ear infection to a sore throat to a case of walking pneumonia—and repeat them all over again. When I complained of an earache, Mom would chase me around the house with the darkest, grossest bottle of medicine I could imagine. After successfully pinning me down, she'd pour the nasty stuff into each ear, which gurgled and churned as it did its germ-destroying work.

As we battled my other sicknesses, my mom also learned that I didn't have a functioning pancreas, a breakdown known as exocrine pancreatic insufficiency, or EPI. What this meant was that my body didn't secrete the digestive enzymes necessary to properly digest food. As a result, my body couldn't absorb the nutrients it needed, which led to issues like diarrhea, loss of appetite, and weight loss. Basically, I was malnourished, which contributed to how sickly I was. We learned soon enough that I had juvenile diabetes, also known as Type 1 diabetes, and I would have to start receiving insulin shots as well as consuming replacement enzymes. My father was always complaining about what it was costing him to take me to the doctor, while my mother defended me, saying it wasn't my fault that I wasn't a perfectly healthy child.

The summer between first and second grade, I suffered another traumatic incident that ranked right up there with getting chomped by Death. When I got out of school, we didn't have money to go on vacation or do anything fun outside of Cleveland, but we did have several beaches on Lake Erie that weren't too far to drive to.

One hot summer day, we were cooling off at Edgewater Beach. After we frolicked in the water, Mom handed me a quarter.

"You can go get yourself a hot dog," she said.

I was shocked. I never got special treats like that. We always picnicked to save money.

There was a hamburger stand on the boardwalk that I set my sights on. While walking through the soft sand, I was focused on the hamburger stand, so I didn't see the bottom half of a broken Coke bottle on the ground in my path. I stepped on it, and the bottle shredded the sole of my left foot.

I fell to the sand. Every nerve in my foot cried out in pain. Mom was too far away to hear my screams. I started crawling back to my family, trailing a crimson river of blood in the sand. Kids looked at me, and some laughed. Then my mother heard my shrieks and sprinted from the blanket she had thrown on the sand.

"What happened, Skeezix?"

"Mom, I stepped on broken glass!"

And then I showed her the bottom of my foot, which was a bloody mess.

She rushed me to a nearby doctor's clinic and helped me onto the examination table. A kindly doctor in a lab coat walked in and looked at the bottom of my bleeding foot, which was filled with sand, glass, and blood.

"We're going to have to stitch him up," he said, stating the obvious. "Let me have a closer look."

When he touched my swollen foot, the pain was so sharp that I blew every drop of snot within me all over his lab coat. The doctor recoiled, aghast at my involuntary action. Then he did his best to get cleaned up.

"How much is this going to cost?" my mom asked. We didn't have health insurance, so she had to know.

"Around fifty dollars, ma'am."

Fifty dollars was more than Mom had, especially after she had paid all the medical bills to find out why I was so sick all the time.

"We can't afford that," she said.

She thanked the doctor for his time and drove me home, where she drew a bath, plopped me in the water, and raised my injured foot in the air. I was given a rag and told to bite on it because this was going to hurt. Then Mom painstakingly removed each shard of glass and every speck of sand with tweezers as she continually rinsed the area with clean water. The pain was excruciating, and while the rag kept me from screaming, plenty of tears landed in the bathtub that night.

I needed to be stitched up, but that was too expensive and wasn't going to happen. Consequently, my huge gash turned into a huge scar. Even now, if I walk a certain way, I receive a jolt of pain, and when the weather's going to turn, my left foot is the first to know.

• • •

Mom was happy that I liked my first few years of elementary school. She was big on education. She always told me, "If you can read, you can learn. If you can learn, you can be anybody you want to be."

My thirst for learning was sparked at a young age by the gift of a used set of Childcraft encyclopedias—fifteen volumes in all. With simple, descriptive sentences and plenty of vivid, eye-popping illustrations, the encyclopedia set was created for young children like me. Mom would let me crawl into bed with one of the volumes and read to me until I fell asleep. That made me feel close to her.

Each encyclopedia had a certain smell of cotton—something clean, something good. Every time I opened up one of the gilt-edged volumes, the crisp pages produced a cracking sound. The glossy layouts were amazing and captured my eye.

I read about how candy was made. How tornadoes happen. When dinosaurs roamed the earth. The meteorites in the night sky. What the Reformation and industrial revolution were all about. I must have thumbed through every page of those fifteen volumes. Reading the Childcraft encyclopedias felt like a trip to the land of Oz. It seemed like the rest of my world was black and white, but when I opened the pages of a Childcraft encyclopedia, I was drawn into a magical world of color. I was captivated by the interesting information as much as by the photos and illustrations. My imagination soared, and I felt like I was learning so much.

Mom was a font of encouragement every time I held a Childcraft volume in my hands. One night before bed she told me, "Reading those encyclopedias is part of getting a good education, which will allow you to go places I could never go. Sometimes I had to do what I had to do, but you can do better. A good education will help you become independent."

I knew education was important to Mom because she was going to night school three nights a week, but an adult going to school seemed odd to me.

"Why are you going to school?" I asked her one evening as she was gathering her textbooks and notes after dinner.

"Because I never finished high school," she said.

"How come you never finished high school?"

My mother paused. "Well, I had to take care of your aunts and uncles, but I also had to work nights. I was the oldest, you know. So I dropped out. But there's no way you're not going to finish school, young man. I don't want you missing out like I did."

Mom tried to make up for her lack of a formal education by reading. There was always a stack of books on her nightstand—titles like *To Kill a Mockingbird* by Harper Lee or *The Death of a President* by William Manchester. She loved reading and also enjoyed listening to classical music on the stereo hi-fi in our living room. Looking back, I'm surprised my father—Professor Higgins—didn't think much of my mother's pursuit of learning, but he did share her enjoyment of classical music. He and Mom glided across the living room floor to Tchaikovsky's "Nutcracker Suite" and Beethoven's "Für Elise" and "Moonlight Sonata." They sang along with Julie Andrews on *The Sound of Music*.

But everything always circled back to reading. Mom would tell me, "Of all the investments you can make in life, reading will never disappoint you. You can buy a house, but they can take that away from you. You can buy a car, but they can take that away from you. You can buy clothing, but clothing wears out. But once you get an education, nobody can repossess it. Nobody can come to your house and claim it."

Mom cared so much about education because becoming independent was a big theme for her.

"Skeezix, I want you to be your own man when you grow up," she would tell me. "I want you to be independent. I never want to see you crippled emotionally or physically. You have to watch and learn from what's happening around you."

Mom was what people in the inner city called "street smart." She was aware of her surroundings and was quick to act when she saw opportunity. Mom wanted to teach me that as well, but she sure had a funny way of doing so.

Once she took Crystal and me to a local fast-food restaurant. She ordered us their dollar special—a greasy hamburger, large fries, and a Coke.

We accepted the bags of food Mom gave us and sat down in a booth. Mom faced us—and the kitchen.

We were enjoying our food when suddenly there was a lot of commotion. People started running out of the restaurant in a panic. Mom's eyes darted about. The next thing I knew, she grabbed her purse and ran toward the rear exit. She left in such a hurry that my sister and I weren't sure what to do. We stayed in our booth as if we were statues. Mom hadn't said goodbye or told us anything.

"What's she doing?" Crystal asked.

"I don't know," I replied, as mystified as my sister.

The restaurant was emptying out as smoke filled the seating area, but we remained frozen in our seats, not knowing what to do.

Then a man in a white uniform and chef's toque ran up to us. "C'mon, we have no time to lose!" He boosted Crystal into his arms and extended his free hand to me. Then the man led us out the back of the restaurant and reunited my sister and me with Mom.

It was when we were together that I saw the kitchen was on fire. Sirens wailed, and then we watched a battalion of firemen attack the blaze. The fire didn't burn the restaurant down, but we witnessed quite a conflagration.

"Time to go," my mother announced.

"Mom, why didn't you save us?" I wondered aloud on our way to the car.

"Fool, if you see me running, you better be running too."

Translation: *I'm getting out of here, and you're old enough to save yourselves. You better watch and learn.*

That was classic Ma.

Mom may not have had much formal education, but she had a way of figuring things out. Nobody knew how to stretch a dollar better than she did—and she had to do that often because Dad controlled the finances in the family and didn't give her much to spend. One way of stretching her money involved shopping at thrift stores, but not just any thrift stores. She recognized that Goodwill and Salvation Army stores in the better neighborhoods were the best places to shop for clothes because their inventory of donated clothes came from the wealthiest communities. She could buy the nicest gently used clothing for pennies on the dollar when compared to retail.

She always said, "You can be poor, but you can still wear nice, clean, fashionable clothes." I can remember her taking us to fancy, multistory department stores on lower Euclid Avenue like Higbee's and Halle Brothers, where she would point out current fashions. Then she'd drive us to a Goodwill near an affluent neighborhood like Bentleyville or Hunting Valley and show us the same fashions for a tenth of the price, meaning a thirty-dollar pair of barely worn dress shoes might be two or three bucks in the thrift shop. She would say that clothing stores always have something to sell you, but you don't have to buy unless the price is right.

She applied the same value proposition to doctors. When she had money in her pocket, she'd pack us up in her Corvair and drive us to the wealthier suburbs to see doctors who practiced in the middle- and upper-class neighborhoods belonging to the white folk. Mom was always thinking of ways to do things better and beyond her current reality.

Even though money was almost always tight at home, there were two occasions she saved up for—Christmas and birthdays. She picked up the Christmas spirit from Grannie, who always put on a German-style *Weihnachten,* complete with a Christmas tree lit with real candles and all the trappings of a European Christmas.

Mom made sure we got a good tree and would have Crystal and me help her decorate its branches while the "Nutcracker Suite" played in the background. Mom occasionally liked to hide presents around the house and direct us to find them through a series of "you're getting hot" and "you're getting cold" directions. One Christmas morning, she directed me to our cold garage, where I found something really hot waiting for me—a new bike!

Mom went crazy with Christmas presents, big and small, and she stacked them under the tree, which only contributed to the magic of Christmas in this kid's eyes. There were so many presents that it felt like I was in the middle of a fairyland.

One year, she told us she had recorded Santa Claus when he climbed down the chimney with his sackful of presents.

As a small kid, I lapped it up. "Really? What did he say?" I asked.

Mom had an old reel-to-reel tape recorder. She flipped it on, and I heard a husky-sounding voice saying, "Ho, ho, ho, look at these sugar cookies they left me" and "I wonder if Ronaldo and Crystal have been good this year."

I was so sure Santa was speaking that I didn't recognize Mom's voice. She must have been repressing a laugh as she watched me listen to "Santa" muse about this and that. I certainly didn't catch on.

The other big day of the year was our birthdays. Even though Mom could be tough on me the rest of the year, she made sure my birthday was really special. She always gave me a party with family members and friends and a birthday cake and lit candles (one for each year). There were party hats, streamers, and plenty of presents.

The reason I share these stories about my mother is to show how Christmas and birthdays were a big part of her German American background and her personality. Giving gifts on these two days of the year was her love language. She wasn't a hugger, a kisser, or an affectionate person because she had trained herself to stuff her emotions down. For 363 days a year, she was hard, tough, and unemotional with me, but she found it within herself to open up her heart on Christmas and my birthday.

Looking back, I can say that Mom tried the best she could with the tools she had, blunted as they were.

3

TRIPPING OVER WORDS

As much as I liked reading, as much as I liked learning, and as much as I liked white teachers, I sure didn't like speaking in public.

That's because I stuttered.

Now, there are those who stutter here and there, stumbling over certain words or sounds but eventually working their way through what they want to say. Not me. I was a *severe* stutterer. I tripped over words as if both my sneakers were tied together.

I didn't know that stuttering was a developmental speech disorder that usually presents itself between the ages of three and eight before getting worked out sometime during puberty. All I knew was that my throat constricted and my tongue turned to Jell-O whenever I was called upon in the classroom.

I can't remember when I started stuttering, but it became a big problem during my early primary school years. If called upon in class, I was sure to stammer like a cartoon character—and hear snickers from the other students. My face would flush with embarrassment every time, so I clammed up. I wouldn't raise my hand to answer a teacher's question. No way, no how.

On the first day of fourth grade, my new teacher stood at the door to welcome each student. My heart skipped a beat. She was a beautiful young black teacher who introduced herself as Miss Johnson. Her resemblance to actress Diahann Carroll, who starred in the TV sitcom *Julia*, was uncanny.

"Your name, young man?"

"Rrrrr . . . Ron Archer," I croaked. Already I was off to a bad start, and I wanted to impress Miss Johnson badly. I had an instant crush on her.

Miss Johnson consulted her seating plan. "Welcome, Master Archer. I'm seating everyone alphabetically. You're in the first row next to the window with the A's and the B's. Please take the fourth desk."

The classroom filled rapidly. All my classmates were black—some lighter, some darker than me. When we were settled, Miss Johnson addressed the class.

"Listen up, everyone. I would like each of you to stand up and tell the classroom what you did during your summer vacation," she said. "We'll start with our first row."

I groaned. I knew when it was my turn that I would stand up and stammer, and that's when the teasing would start.

The kid in front of me was Jimmy Andrews. When it was his turn, he took the floor with confidence. He was funny and smooth and handsome—everything I was not. I was dying inside because I knew I would have to follow his silver tongue. My heart pounded in my chest, and my palms were rivers of sweat. Listening to Jimmy was pure torture. My throat and tongue swelled like a sponge full of water.

While my classmates laughed at his funny stories, I felt like a man blindfolded in front of a firing squad, just waiting to hear the cocking of guns, the pulling of triggers, and the firing of shots. When Jimmy sat down, I could hear my heart beating through my ears.

Miss Johnson looked at her seating chart. "Master Archer, now it's your turn," she said. "Can you start by telling us your first name?"

I stood up and wiped my clammy hands on my pants. I opened my mouth and formed my lips and tongue to speak, but nothing came out. My jaw locked and my chest tightened so hard that I could hardly breathe. I had an anxiety attack. I felt like I was sinking in quicksand with a python wrapped around my neck and squeezing with everything it had.

Finally an utterance came out, but it sounded more like an old car trying to start up on a cold winter's day.

"Rrrrr . . . Rrrrr . . . Rrrrr . . ."

A minute of trying to say *Ronaldo* seemed like an hour. I didn't want to give up, but I couldn't pronounce my name for the life of me.

"That's enough, Master Archer. Please sit down and be quiet."

That's all the inducement my classmates needed to laugh at me as if they were listening to Bob Hope entertaining the troops at Christmas. Loud giggling filled the classroom, and I felt like I was shrinking to the size of a chipmunk. If only there were a hole for me to crawl into and die.

After that, I refused to speak up and participate in class lessons, which impacted my grades. I was sure Miss Johnson thought I was behind a grade level.

That's exactly what she must have thought, because she informed my principal that I was a dysfunctional kid who was holding my class back. The principal ordered me to be removed from my mainstream class and become part of a special-education group that met in a dark, dank, windowless room of the school basement that was noisy as heck because it was next door to the boiler room.

The humiliation crushed me.

• • •

Each morning, I trudged down the concrete stairs to a dark room with no windows, no artwork on the walls, no motivational posters, and no cut-out clouds filled with pithy sayings. I sat at a low desk with several other students and either finger painted or glued pieces of uncooked macaroni onto a piece of paper and into the shapes of people, cars, and towns.

I knew exactly what was going on, but I was powerless to change my plight. Even my mother, with her strong emphasis on education, was powerless in this situation. In those days, and especially in my black community, there were four authority figures who were never questioned—pastors, principals, teachers, and nurses—so there was little sense in arguing.

I was stuck. All day long . . . finger painting and macaroni crafts. I couldn't wait until I got home so I could read my Childcraft encyclopedias and receive some real academic nourishment.

But going home after school presented a challenge because sooner or later, my father would show up at the front door, loaded for bear. Whatever the reason for his foul mood, it didn't take him long to blow a fuse and lose his temper with Mom—or with me.

Tied to my constant illnesses, I was a mess. I started wetting my bed each night.

One morning, my father came in to check on me. He had heard Mom complain about having to change the sheets and run a new load of laundry day after day.

I woke up as I heard him brusquely open my bedroom door. *Oops.* Everything was wet.

"You peed in the bed again? What's wrong with you?" my father demanded.

He jerked the covers off, which revealed a damp stain the size of a hubcap underneath my frame. My pajama bottoms were soaked as well.

If I said anything, I would incur even more wrath. I readied myself for the back of his hand.

"The next time you pee in the bed, I'm going to wrap these sheets around you and send you to school like the pee-boy you are!"

I believed the threat, but that didn't stop me from wetting the bed.

Years later, I would learn that I was a bed wetter because my underdeveloped bladder was too small for my body since I was born a month prematurely. When you couple the physical reasons for having a small bladder with the emotional trauma I experienced at school and in the home, you have a recipe for wetting the bed every night, which frustrated my mother to no end.

And my mother's frustrations spilled over into her marriage. She and my father argued a lot—from why he was gone so much to the need for a better and bigger car to plain old personality clashes.

My father didn't like it when she stood up for herself, so there was violence between them. Since he couldn't control her intellectually—my mom could be quite verbal when the occasion warranted it—his only way to get back at her was to strike her with his closed fist and inflict sharp physical pain.

I saw him resort to hideous violence many times. My father's huge hands were lined with veins that stood out like strands of rope. He pummeled my mother like a man beating another man; it was brutal to watch because I was powerless to rescue her.

And when he felt like he couldn't get the upper hand with Mom, my father beat me for the slightest infraction. Or whenever he felt like it.

My father exuded a coldness near me that made me afraid. When he was with me, he never smiled. This was baffling, because when he was with my sister, he would smile.

I would see my father interact with Crystal, and he was happy and joking. With me, he was cold and hard and distant and

dismissive and uncaring. I couldn't understand why he was physically rough with me, even in the way he tickled me. Whenever he
tickled Crystal, she laughed like a hyena, but whenever he tickled
me, he would dig his strong fingers into my ribs in a way that
caused deep pain, not laughter. My ribs would hurt so much that
I could hardly breathe deeply the next day.

Just hearing him sneeze was enough for me to pee in my pants.
I was terrified by the power in that man's body. When he blew
a fuse, he'd scream and holler, which I knew was a precursor
to a good whack or two. I felt like I was living with a lion and I was
covered in a meat suit. Any minute he would turn on me and
devour me.

He made it clear that I was never good enough. He never said
those words, but I sure felt those sentiments. My father was never
proud of me, never happy for me. He never said "I love you" to me,
but I bet I heard him make that simple statement of affection to
my sister every day.

My younger sister, Crystal, wasn't doing me any favors either.
Simply put, she was a tattletale, and if she could get me into trouble, she was happy to do so.

I got blamed for everything—the toys being left out, the open
milk bottle on the kitchen table, the front door being left open.

"He did it, Daddy!"

I'd run upstairs to my room whenever I heard her cast the
blame on me. Her word was golden. She was judge and jury.

One day I was in my bedroom, lying on my bed and reading
a book, when I heard Crystal talking to my dad in the bathroom
we shared.

"Daddy, the sink won't work," she said.

I heard water hitting the sink. "You're right, it's blocked up,"
my father said. There was an edge to his voice. I'm sure he was
thinking about how much it would cost to get a plumber over
to the house to fix the backed-up sink.

"What happened?" he asked.

"Skeezix was playing with his Matchbox cars and let one fall into the sink. That's why the water won't go down," Crystal replied.

The next thing I knew, my bedroom door burst open. My father grabbed me by the scruff of the neck and flung me to the floor. Then he beat me like a dog.

"You—" *Thump* "—stupid—" *Thump* "—idiot!" *Thump*. *Thump*. "How many times—" *Thump* "—do I have to—" *Thump* "—whip your butt—" *Thump* "—to get it through your thick skull?" *Thump. Thump.*

Between blows, I looked toward the doorway. My sister, two years younger than me, stood there watching, knowing I was being punished for her crime. But she didn't say a word.

I curled up in a ball to protect myself as best I could, but resistance was futile. When my father got tired of beating me, I looked at my sister again. She was still smirking in the doorway. I thought, *How could you ever do this to anyone, let alone your brother?*

I never got an answer to my question because I could never ask it. I couldn't risk confronting my sister. She held the power because my father believed everything she said.

No, it was best to lie low, as low as I could, and hope my sister would tire of the sport.

My father was a volcano, and I never knew when the next eruption would occur.

Once we were sitting at the kitchen table, pouring breakfast cereal into our bowls and getting ready to eat when my dad said, "Everybody, let's say a prayer for Linda today."

And then he bowed his head and mumbled, "Be with Linda today, Lord, and keep her on the straight and narrow."

First of all, we never prayed before meals. Second, we never went to church, so this was completely out of place. And now my father wanted to pray for someone named Linda? I had no idea what he was doing or who he was referring to.

Mom exploded. She grabbed the kitchen table and flipped it over, sending boxes of cereal, cups of coffee, glasses of orange juice, and a carton of milk to the linoleum floor.

"Maybe you need to tell Linda to pray for *us*!" she screamed. "You jerk!"

My father wasn't going to take that sitting down. He jumped up and grabbed her by the neck, lifting her out of her seat and tossing her to the floor like a Raggedy Ann doll. Crystal and I ran like rats out of the kitchen. When I looked back, my father was beating my mother with his fists.

Mom ran out to the living room, and I could see the terror in her face. My father bore down on her. After several more blows, he took off his belt. She put up her arms to block the belt, but he was too fast for her. She couldn't fend off every blow, and she eventually slumped to the floor, where he kept pummeling her.

He stopped to catch his breath. "You have nowhere to go!" he taunted her. "Without me, you'll be back on the streets in no time!"

I wasn't sure what he meant by that. She'd have to sleep outside, with no home to go to?

My father put his belt back on with a look of satisfaction.

Then he looked across the living room and saw me.

I didn't want to be next. I ran upstairs to my room, hoping his frustration was spent.

•   •   •

Shortly after I turned ten, there was complete turmoil in our home. I witnessed physical fights between my parents every few days. It didn't take much for my father to blow a fuse about something—a car breakdown, Mom not waiting for him to arrive for dinner, or some purchase that he didn't like. Anything out of the ordinary, and Dad would blow his stack.

Sometimes he would give Mom a piece of his mind, but other times he would skip the verbal tirade and hit her with clenched fists. Mom would yell at him, "Keep your hands off of me!" but that was like waving a red cape in front of a charging bull.

One early evening, on a Friday, my father upped the ante on the violence. I was in my bedroom upstairs when I heard the awful sounds of a strong man striking a smaller woman over and over in their bedroom.

Whack. "Take that, woman!" *Whack*. "There's more of that coming!" *Whack*. On and on the beating continued.

I set down my Childcraft volume and listened. The sounds of muffled thumps through the wall twisted my stomach. Whatever was driving my father's rage was not satisfied by the physical pain he was inflicting on my mother. Her protests weakened with each blow until she was mute.

I felt like I could do nothing to help Mom or save her. My father was twice my size, so even if I stood between him and my mother, he'd have no problem pushing me aside to get to Mom. Of that I was sure.

Finally, I heard him exit their bedroom and tromp down the stairs. I looked out my bedroom window and saw him driving away. The last time that had happened, I remembered Mom telling me that my father cooled off at the local tavern with a few beers.

Silence filled the house. I tiptoed out of my bedroom. I listened for Crystal, but she didn't make a sound from her bedroom.

I walked down the hall to the master bedroom and found Mom sitting on the edge of her bed, sniffling with her head down. When she looked up, what I saw made me nauseous. Blood dripped from a corner of her mouth. Her cheeks were red and puffy. Her nose looked disjointed, like it was broken. Her left eye was nearly swollen shut, and the way her face was tilted, I wondered if her jaw was broken. Her right arm had been shredded by my father's belt buckle again—it was covered with more than a half dozen fleshy gouges.

This beautiful creature who was my mother looked as if she'd been in a car wreck where the Jaws of Life were needed to save her.

Just as quickly, Mom dropped her head and started crying. I approached and sat down next to her. I put my arm around her and leaned close.

"I'm s-s-sorry, Mommy." I was practically in tears.

"Not as sorry as your father is going to be." Her words were barely a whisper, but there was a steely determination to them.

She pulled herself together and walked downstairs to our phone in the living room.

She placed a call to her sister Ann.

I eavesdropped on the conversation from the second-story landing.

"Yeah, Ann, it's me. That insane monster did it again. He beat me like a dog."

Mom spoke like a defeated woman, her voice sad and gloomy. She listened for a moment to my aunt, who likely offered soothing words. Then I heard Mom say, "Yeah, I know I don't sound too good. But that's going to be the last time he lays hands on me. You still with me?"

Mom listened some more. They seemed to be agreeing on something.

Mom thanked her sister. "See you tomorrow night," she said. Then she set the phone back on its cradle.

Something about our miserable lives had to change, but nothing could have prepared me for what was coming next.

4
—

THINGS FALL APART

'll never forget the following evening, a Friday. Crystal was spending the night at a friend's house. Aunt Ann came over for a quiet dinner of fried chicken, mashed potatoes, and collard greens cooked in bacon grease and sweet onions.

Mom could always cook up a storm. She had a lot of experience around a kitchen stove because when she was growing up, the cooking duties fell on her—the oldest child—since Grannie had to work to provide for the family. Mom's Southern fried chicken was my absolute favorite meal, and my mother knew it. On this particular evening, she fried drumsticks and set the crispy pieces in a small basket with a red-and-white checkered cloth. With the aroma of fried chicken coming from the kitchen, I couldn't help but sneak into the kitchen and grab a piece.

Mom saw me pinch a drumstick and smiled slyly. I tiptoed out of the kitchen with my little snack, loving every crunchy bite.

Normally, Mom would have used her stern voice to tell me to wait until dinner, but on this evening, she gave me a conspiratorial wink. This would be our little secret.

When Aunt Ann arrived, Mom said dinner was ready.

"Where's Dad?" I asked. Normally, Mom waited for him to get home from work before serving dinner.

"He called and said he was working late and we should eat without him," Mom replied.

I shrugged my shoulders. Nothing was consistent in my life, especially mealtimes. But after we sat down for dinner, I noticed that Mom and Aunt Ann seemed to be on edge—as nervous as cats in a room full of rocking chairs.

Something was up.

After clearing the dishes, Mom thanked me for helping out. I went upstairs to resume reading my Childcraft encyclopedias. I loved being transported to areas outside my world through the power of reading. Around seven o'clock, I heard a car drive up. I looked out my second-story window. In the twilight hour, I saw my father step out of the car, puffing one of his cigars.

I had a feeling something was going to blow. Maybe it was the knowing looks that Mom and Aunt Ann exchanged or the way conversation seemed forced that night. If there was going to be fireworks, I wanted to witness how things went down. Maybe I could help my mother if the situation got out of hand.

I tiptoed out of my bedroom and took a seat on the stairs. I looked down at my mother, who sat in a living room chair that faced the front door. And then I saw the shock of my life: in her lap, her hands cradled a handgun. And Aunt Ann sat on a nearby couch with a shotgun across her legs!

Fear rose in my throat—fear that something horrible was going to happen. Why had my parents' marriage deteriorated this far? I figured Mom would threaten my father and tell him to keep his hands off her—or face the consequences.

I heard my father step on the wooden porch and approach the front door. Aunt Ann moved from the couch and took a spot on the floor next to my mother. Then my aunt aimed her shotgun at the front door.

My mother examined the handgun. Satisfied that her gun was loaded, she smoothed the hem of her dress and waited for my father's entry. This was going to be an ambush!

My heart was in my throat. Was Mom actually going to shoot Dad? Was this really happening? I felt like I was an eyewitness to something unbelievable.

My father opened the front door and stepped inside. Sporting a big mustache and a slight Afro, he adjusted his thick eyeglasses as he stepped over the threshold. He held a black briefcase in his left hand, and a thick cigar hung from his mouth.

What happened next was like a slow-motion scene in the movies.

My father's cigar nearly dropped out of his mouth when he saw Mom pointing a gun at him from her chair.

My mother kept her revolver trained on my father. "I am the last woman you are ever going to beat up," she announced.

With that pronouncement, she stood up, planted her feet, extended her arms, and fired her handgun, which created a deafening noise. The loud crack reverberated through the house. I jerked; I had never heard a gunshot before.

The average bullet travels at 2,500 feet per second, or 1,700 miles per hour. In my mother's situation, the bullet traveled the twenty feet in eight one-thousandths of a second, which was not enough time for my father to duck.

It turned out that Friday was his lucky day: the bullet creased his Afro and created a new part in his curly hair before lodging in the wooden doorjamb immediately behind him. (That bullet hole can still be seen today at my mother's house.)

In other words, the bullet missed his skull by millimeters and passed through his frizzy mane, creating the pungent smell of burning hair.

Mom must have been so shocked that she actually pulled the trigger that she couldn't fire a second time. The momentary reprieve gave my father the opportunity to hightail it out of the house. I ran back to my room, where I watched him pop open the trunk of his car. There he found what he was looking for—a handgun. He looked to see if it was loaded.

Now I really didn't know what would happen, but I thought he was going to kill my mother.

I returned to the stairs in time to see my mother and Aunt Ann taking cover next to the front door, which was halfway open. The next thing I knew, Mom fired off another shot in the general direction of my father.

I ran back to my room and saw my father perched behind his car. "That crazy woman is trying to kill me!" he screamed to no one in particular.

Mom got off several more shots, keeping my father pinned.

Then the shooting stopped.

I ran back to the stairs and saw my mother reloading. Aunt Ann brandished her shotgun, but she didn't fire.

The break in the action was all my father needed to jump into his car and speed away.

Now what was going to happen?

Part of me didn't want to stick around to find out. I hustled back to my room but heard muffled voices coming from the living room.

"If he comes back, I'll finish him off."

"No, you won't. I think you've taken things far enough. I'm sure the cops will be here any minute."

Sure enough, within ten minutes I heard sirens. I returned to my perch and saw two cop cars pull up to the house and double-park. By this time, there were a bunch of kids and adults standing on the sidewalk across the street because the gunshot blasts had reverberated through the neighborhood.

My father was seated in the back of one of the cruisers. Three cops escorted him to the front door, and Mom and Aunt Ann greeted them and waved them inside. Mom acted surprised to see everyone.

"Is this your husband, ma'am?" one of the officers asked, holding a pad and pencil.

"Yes, he is," she said.

"Ma'am, your husband is reporting that you tried to kill him with a handgun when he came home from work."

"Is that so?" Mom brought her hand to her face, like this was the most unusual thing she had ever heard.

"Yes, that's what he told us."

My mother straightened her dress. "Well, officers, it's like this. This man tried to kill me. Take a look here."

With that, my mother pointed to her black eye, which was still bruised like a peach in late summer. Then she pointed to the gashes on her arms. "He also beat me within an inch of my life, and then he was going to do me in tonight. He has a gun. Check his car. Besides, do I look like I could hurt this man?"

Mom, who was considerably smaller than my father, delivered an Academy Award-worthy performance, and the cops believed her. They put my father under arrest and took him away, but not before he pointed a finger at her and delivered a parting shot: "Woman, you're poor, you're ignorant, and you're uneducated. You won't be able to keep the house. You're going to lose it because I'm going to take it from you. You will go back to the streets where you belong."

My mother stood her ground and didn't say a word.

In the coming days and weeks, it dawned on my mother that she came *this close* to killing another human being. Yes, he had beaten her horribly for years, uttering the meanest things, but did that justify murder? I didn't think so. After all, he was my father, even though he was mean to me.

At my grandmother's one night, I heard Mom say that if she had been sitting down when she fired her gun, the bullet would have gone through his forehead. But because she stood up and immediately fired her weapon, her aim was off just enough to zip through his Afro instead of penetrating his skull and killing him.

My mother wasn't charged for attempted murder, but her relationship with Dick Archer was over. And she worried that my father would return to kill her. Mom kept the front door bolted and placed an ironing board against the back door so he couldn't break in. She also kept her handgun loaded and in her nightstand in case he ever came back to harm us.

This was a dark, dark time. The only family I had ever known had broken up. Without my father's income, we were soon low on food and eating potato soup every night. I was finger painting all day at school and not learning anything. I was teased in the schoolyard as "Renardo the Retardo."

But that was just the tip of the iceberg.

•   •   •

Around the time of my parents' worsening marriage, my mother would have a neighborhood woman watch me on Friday afternoons. I'll call her Mrs. Brown. What I'm about to describe will be difficult to read, but I can assure you that it's even more difficult to share.

Mom had recently gotten a job as a nurse's aide at the local veterans hospital and had to work longer on Fridays. I don't know why Crystal didn't join me. Perhaps she had a friend who said she could come over to her house after school. I didn't have that type of friend.

Mrs. Brown was married and had three children who were a few years older than me. She had this thing about being "clean." She was always scrubbing pots and pans in the kitchen and washing clothes and hanging them up in her basement.

"You have to be clean," she said one time as she scoured an iron skillet with steel wool. "Being clean is really important. We're going to have to clean your backside."

Mrs. Brown had a friend with her, another woman her age, and they exchanged a knowing look.

"I'm already cl-cl-clean," I said. "I t-t-t-take a bath every day."

"No, I'm sure that backside of yours isn't clean," Mrs. Brown insisted. "This is what I want you to do. I want you to go down into the basement and take off your clothes. Mrs. Jackson and I will arrive shortly and get you clean."

"B-b-b-but I don't want to—"

"You will do what I say, young man. Now march."

There didn't seem to be any way I could get out of this. "Okay," I said.

"And be sure to take off your underwear, too. We need to get you clean."

Maybe she is going to wash my clothes, I thought. Her washer was in the basement, just like in our house. It was one of those old-style washers with a hand-cranked ringer above the open tub. When the washing cycle was over, you ran your clothes through the ringer to squeeze out the extra moisture. Then you could hang the clothes up to dry.

I went downstairs into the basement, lit by a single bulb in the middle of the room. I took off all my clothes and waited, thinking the entire time, *This is the weirdest thing I've ever been asked to do, but I'm just a kid, and they're adults.*

Mrs. Jackson arrived first, followed by Mrs. Brown, who held a broomstick in her right hand.

Everything that happened next was a blur. What I remember is Mrs. Jackson tackling me and pinning me to the concrete floor.

"Spread 'em!" Mrs. Brown barked.

The end of the broomstick had been shaved into a point. She jammed the end of the broomstick into a place where the sun don't shine . . . and turned it, and turned it, and turned it.

"You need to be clean, young man!" Mrs. Brown's voice had risen several octaves. She seemed to be enjoying this.

Me? I felt like I was being plumbed, but something told me that crying wouldn't do me any good. "Just stop, please!" I grimaced through clenched teeth. "I'll be better! I'll be clean! I'll be nice to others!"

This type of awful abuse happened once a week for six months. After each episode, I was in tremendous pain, but I didn't tell my mom or any adults what was happening. I was sure they would never believe me—and even if Mom did, I thought she would just tell me to be strong. If I was feeling sorry for myself, Mom would often tell me, "There are no crutches in this house." There was no room to be weak and vulnerable, so I suffered in silence.

One time, though, my mother noticed during bath time that I was bleeding from my rectum. She had no idea why that was happening, but she knew what she saw wasn't good.

She rushed me to the emergency room, where a doctor examined me. These days, an emergency room physician would take one look at a bleeding rectum and consider whether this happened because of sexual abuse. But back in the early 1970s, the doctor was flummoxed. He had to do something, so he ordered that my stomach be pumped and gave me some medicine. When I left the hospital, I was given a pat on the head, and that was it.

I was learning what toughness was all about. You don't complain. You don't cry. You don't talk about what's wrong. You keep it to yourself.

I mentioned before that Mrs. Brown had three children. They were older than me, but I learned later that when they reached their teen years, they all became drug addicts. Their short lives did not end well.

All these years later, I feel sorry for them. But while their mother was abusing me, I only felt sorry for myself.

What happened to me in Mrs. Brown's basement created a horror show in my mind. But I felt like I had nobody to help me, nobody to rescue me. Out of a sense of discouragement as well as emotional trauma, I started banging my head against the wall when I went to bed as a way to deal with the emotional pain I felt.

I was a mess. Not only was I being sexually violated by sadistic adults and stuttering like crazy at school, but I was still wetting my bed every night.

I hated waking up. That's when I'd feel the wet spot in my bed and realize nothing had changed.

•   •   •

Things weren't the same after my parents separated. Mom was uptight most of the time, so it didn't take much to tick her off. She complained about how much things cost: food, clothes, and gas. With my father living elsewhere, the three of us were on our own.

We got government assistance, though. Mom wasn't embarrassed at all to sign up for food stamps, a federal program that wasn't available when her father was sentenced to prison. She viewed food stamps as the government providing a safety net so that we could feed ourselves and stay in our home.

Our two-story brick Tudor home was situated in a working-class, predominantly black neighborhood known as Lee-Harvard. Even though the houses and apartments were on the threadbare side, homeowners took pride in their surroundings, no matter how humble. Lawns were mowed, leaves were raked, and sidewalks were hosed down.

Lee-Harvard was known as a "turning neighborhood" even though the exodus of white families that had begun in the early 1960s was nearly complete. Our neighborhood was safe—or at least safe enough for me to ride my bike to a nearby park to play with my friends or join a pickup game on the basketball court. I'm sure Mom let me come and go unattended because she wanted me to burn off some energy in the fresh air.

Hanging out with boys my age is how I learned about the birds and the bees. That's the streets for you. Mom never said a peep to me about sex, although I overheard her and Aunt Ann talking about men in funny ways and how much money you could get out of them. One time I heard Mom say, "You have to pay to play." But I didn't understand what she was talking about.

As for my father sitting down and having "the talk" with me, that wasn't going to happen. Before my parents separated, he hadn't taken much interest in what I did or who I was anyway, so why would he carve out one-on-one time with me to talk about the physical differences between men and women and how babies were made?

So I learned about sex the old-fashioned way: in the gutter.

Even though the anatomical aspect was interesting and I was noticing that girls had appealing curves, I didn't really understand what sex was all about. But then I received a lesson about sex that no boy my age should learn. Once again, this story is very disturbing to read and to share.

On most weekends, my father would arrive Saturday mornings and drive Crystal an hour south to Canton, where his side of the family was from. She got to spend the night with our cousins and have fun while I stayed home. They played games and ate popcorn and stayed up late watching TV. I was jealous.

Aunt Ann usually came over for dinner with us and stayed to babysit me because Mom went out every Saturday night—alone. I thought it was a bit strange that no one ever came to pick her up, and I wondered where she went and who she saw. Mom usually wore a nice navy-blue dress with white pearls around her neck. If the weather was cold, she'd wrap a fashionable shawl around her neck and carry a black leather strapless purse.

When she got all dolled up like that, I thought she looked like Jackie Kennedy. She certainly carried herself like a first lady. Very classy. Almost regal. My mom was a beautiful woman with dark hair, huge eyes, distinctive eyebrows, and a perfect smile. Whenever she took me out shopping, I saw heads turn and guys give her long looks. She certainly was exotic looking for that day and age, which was only natural because she was the daughter of a black man and a white woman.

When Aunt Ann couldn't babysit me on Saturday nights, however, Mom would drive me to a neighbor's house and have her look after me.

This neighbor had three sons and a live-in nanny to take care of her boys because she worked different shifts. The nanny was a fun, outgoing guy. I thought he was a great dresser in flower-power bell-bottoms and long-sleeved paisley shirts. But what happened one evening is forever etched in my memory.

The neighbor was working the swing shift, so the nanny looked after us. It was getting close to bedtime when he said, "Let's go up to the attic."

The other boys seemed to know what was going on, but I was clueless.

"How come we're going to the attic?" I asked.

"Oh, you'll see," the nanny said.

We climbed up to the attic, which had a big mattress on the floor and several fluffy pillows amid boxes and other junk.

"Let's take off our clothes," he said.

I didn't like how that sounded.

"What are we doing?" I asked.

"We're going to play 'naked games,'" the nanny replied.

"But what if I don't want to play?" Even at the age of ten, I didn't like how this was sounding.

"That's okay," he said. "You can watch us."

It seems surreal to describe what happened next, but the three boys and the nanny stripped off all their clothes. I'd never seen a grown man fully naked before, especially one who was aroused.

I watched as he lathered baby oil on my friends' bodies, enjoying every moment.

"Are you sure you don't want to join us, Ronaldo?" he asked.

"Ah, no." This didn't look good. Maybe it helped that I had an independent streak.

"Suit yourself, young man."

And then I watched him do the most unspeakable things with those boys.

I wasn't sexually abused that night, but I was left with indelible memories that I can't shake even to this day.

I didn't tell Mom about the "naked games." At an age when most kids are still fairly innocent to the ways of the world, I learned four things: You don't talk. You don't trust. You don't feel. And you pretend that nothing happened because nobody would believe you anyway.

That's why I couldn't tell Mom what happened. She continued to drop me off at this babysitter's, and if the nanny announced it was time for "naked games," I said, "No way, no how." I never went up to that attic again, but the other boys did, which really bothered me.

No wonder I continued to bang my head against the wall at night. It was hard to cope with what I had seen and the images that replayed themselves in my mind.

One time Crystal, who shared a wall with me, came into my bedroom to check on me. "Why are you banging your head on the wall?" she asked.

"Because I want to."

She shrugged her shoulders. "You're weird," she said.

I thumped my head against the wall a lot. I needed a way to escape my thoughts. That's how I fell asleep every night.

If I was particularly distressed, I'd wet my bed again. I knew what was coming next: a look of disgust from my mother followed by another scolding as she ripped off the damp, smelly sheets to put them in the washer in our basement. And then I'd put on a fresh set of clothes and eat a bowl of cold cereal in total silence, contemplating how I didn't want to go to school.

• • •

Six months after the separation, Mom sensed the turmoil I was experiencing because of the second-class treatment I received from my father.

One Saturday evening, after spending the day playing by myself while Crystal visited our cousins in Canton, Mom noticed the glum look on my face as she was putting me to bed.

Mom drew me close. "I have something to tell you," she said.

I looked up at her, tears pooling in my eyes. She stroked my hair to comfort me. That was unusual. My mother almost never showed me genuine affection.

"You know how your father comes to pick up your sister and takes her for the weekend?" she asked.

I nodded. That was one of the things that bothered me so much. It was obvious that he loved her and didn't love me.

Mom cleared her throat and delivered a bombshell. "He's not your father," she whispered.

My life stood still for a moment. This shouldn't have come as a shock to me. Dick Archer had come into my life after I had been living with Grannie for two years and after my mother returned from New York. But I had so far internalized that he was my father that my mother's revelation struck like a thunderbolt.

My father is not my father? Then who is my father?

As if reading my mind, Mom said, "Your real father was killed in Vietnam."

We had this conversation in 1973 as the Vietnam War was winding down. Even at the age of ten, I knew something about the conflict in Vietnam because it was on TV a lot.

I took a long moment to process this new information. *My father was killed in Vietnam? Then my real father must have been a soldier in the US Army. That makes him a hero.*

"Wow, Mom. What happened?"

"Your father was a brave man. He was fighting the Viet Cong in the jungle when he got killed. He died for our country."

Mom smiled as my mind reeled. I believed her—but then I realized that I would never meet my real father. He was dead. And what Mom said confirmed that the man who picked up my sister was not my father. That also made Crystal my half-sister, not my real sister.

While this revelation made it a little easier to accept my estrangement from Dick Archer, my sense of identity crumpled like a house of cards. Without a sense of identity, I had no sense of history, no sense of being somebody. It was like I was a ghost—someone whose life wasn't what it seemed to be. My whole existence had just been turned upside down. I no longer knew who I was because everything I thought was true *wasn't*.

●　　●　　●

Because Mom was working and out of the house a great deal, Aunt Ann babysat me a lot—so much that she was becoming like a second parent to Crystal and me.

I liked Aunt Ann, who looked like an olive-skinned Sicilian and was short at five feet two inches tall. Despite her lack of height, Aunt Ann was quite a basketball player at a time when basketball wasn't popular for girls and young women. She could dribble like nobody's business and spent many hours at the local park playing in pickup games against the guys. She developed a reliable skyhook and an automatic jump shot. Aunt Ann was fearless on and off the court.

At ten years old, I thought anyone in high school or beyond was an adult, but Aunt Ann was only a dozen years older than me, which meant she was in her early twenties. She was around me enough to know that I was a troubled kid, especially after my father moved out. She knew that the kids at school laughed at me and that I lacked friends. Just as she had grown up in a broken home, the cycle was repeating itself.

One Saturday night, after my mother got all dressed up, splashed perfume on her smooth neck, and left the house, my aunt and I got to talking. It was just the two of us since Crystal was with her father, having fun with the cousins in Canton. *Of course he wouldn't take me*, I thought. *I'm not family.*

The revelation that Dick Archer was not my real father consumed me. I'm sure it was written all over my face, which is why my aunt first broached the topic.

"I understand that you know about your real father," Aunt Ann said.

"Yeah, Mom told me."

"Your father was a courageous man," she said. "You can be proud."

My face brightened. Since my father had died in Vietnam, maybe he had been one of the Green Berets I had read about in the Childcraft encyclopedia—the soldiers dressed in camouflage who slip in behind enemy lines to conduct clandestine missions.

I hung on to that thought, but hope turned to fear later that night. I was sleeping when I heard men burst through the front door.

I shot up in bed. Then I heard a dog barking like crazy.

Heavy boots came up the stairs. I shivered in my bed. *Were they going to kill me?*

A door opened, and a bright light flashed in my face. The men were cops!

"She's not here, Miller," one cop said. The door slammed shut.

I heard more rumbling and then a scream—they had found Mom in her bedroom.

Heavy boots passed my door, and as they made their way down the stairs, I stepped out into the hall.

Mom, dressed in a nightgown and a jacket, had her arms behind her back. Silver handcuffs bound her. A German shepherd barked and snarled. I heard one of the cops say, "You're under arrest for solicitation," but I wasn't sure what that meant.

"Mom!" I shouted, terrified.

My mother looked up, defeated.

"Call Aunt Ann!"

One of the cops gave Mom a slight shove in the back with his baton. "Get a move on, lady," he said. They stepped through the front door and were gone.

I ran back into my bedroom and watched one of the cops put his hand on top of her head as he brusquely pushed her into the backseat of the black-and-white.

Red lights flashed on the bar atop the car roof. There was no siren.

As they drove Mom away, I had never felt more alone.

•   •   •

Mom was allowed to come home after a few hours that night, although that didn't stop her Saturday night outings. One Saturday evening after the cops' visit, I found Mom in her bathroom, getting dressed to go out. What I saw shocked me.

Mom didn't look like Mom. She wore a blonde wig with big, soft curls and a slinky cocktail dress. She didn't see me as she leaned toward the mirror and applied black eyeliner.

And then she started singing.

"Happy biiirthdaaay, to you. Happy biiirthdaaay, to you. Happy biiirthdaaay, Mister President. Happy—"

And then she spotted me in the mirror and stopped singing, a bit embarrassed.

"What are you doing, Mom?"

"Just practicing." My mother continued to work a black pencil around the corner of her eye.

I was confused. *Why would Mom want to look like Marilyn Monroe?* I'd seen pictures of the famous Hollywood star in *Life* magazine. I knew she had committed suicide before I was born. What I witnessed made no sense to me.

Each time Mom left the home dressed up for some fancy party, I experienced separation anxiety. My heart ached for her because I had a sinking feeling that something sexual was going on with Mom, and whatever was happening, it was against her will.

I wanted so much to say, *You're so beautiful, Mom. Be careful.* But I could never utter those words. Even if I tried, I'd probably end up stuttering.

Now why would a boy think such thoughts about his mother?

I suppose the answer is that I had been exposed to a great deal on the streets, from what older guys on the basketball court said they did to girls to the horrible things I saw the nanny do to those boys.

It was during this time that I started spending a lot more time in the basement of our house. We had a finished basement that was drafty and cold, but for me, it was my sanctuary. Our basement wasn't huge, just big enough for a couch, a throw rug, a black-and-white TV, and a washer. The basement became a place for me to escape—to hide, to feel safe—and was a metaphor for my life: it was underground, it was hidden, and it was away from the rest of the house. I felt the most comfortable down there because that's where I found peace.

I'd plop on the couch and get lost for hours watching *Looney Tunes.* The characters were my friends: Bugs Bunny. Daffy Duck. Foghorn Leghorn. Road Runner. They fueled my escape.

The antenna on our TV set was broken, but my stepfather had hooked up an old coat hanger as the "rabbit ears" before he moved out. The channel knob was busted, so I had to use a pair of pliers to change to a new station, but I didn't mind. There were only a handful of channels anyway.

My favorite after-school cartoon was *Speed Racer*. The protagonist was known for his love of car racing and his family. He drove the Mach 5. *He* could escape. He could get away from danger, go into water, go over water, cut down trees, jump over the Grand Canyon, get around any obstacle.

I couldn't do any of those things. I was trapped.

But when Speed Racer successfully drove his Mach 5 to get away from extreme danger, I became him, vicariously imagining my own escape.

If there was one thing I liked more than watching cartoons, it was watching cartoons *and* eating ice cream. Mom kept a half gallon of my favorite flavor—chocolate almond—in the stand-up freezer in our basement.

One Friday night when Mom was gone, I helped myself to four big scoops of chocolate almond ice cream. Because the freezer was on a slight slant, you had to slam the door shut or it would remain open. That night, I got my ice cream but didn't slam the door. Eventually, I went to bed.

At three o'clock in the morning, the light to my bedroom switched on. I shielded my eyes from the bright illumination. Then I noticed Mom standing in the door. She was loaded for bear.

"You idiot! How many times have I told you to slam the freezer door!"

A leather belt strap whipped through the air. I raised my arms in time to keep the belt from striking my face, but the blow still stung.

"Get up! To the basement!"

I felt another lash—and another—as I hurried out of the bedroom. I burst into tears and made a run for it. Mom followed me but couldn't keep up.

When I got to the basement, I saw what I had done: the freezer door was wide open, and thawed ice cream had pooled on the concrete floor.

Another lash ripped into my back. I turned and faced Mom with arms upraised as she delivered another blow, and then I ran back upstairs to my bedroom, a jumble of tears and deep anguish.

As I fell asleep that traumatic night, it felt like even my mother had turned on me.

5

—

A DESPONDENT TURN

What brings down a tree?

Is it one final stroke of the ax or the thousand swings before?

All the strokes have an impact in bringing a tree down. It's like what Smokin' Joe Frazier, the heavyweight boxing champion of the world at the time, said about taking out an opponent—that when you kill the body with heavy punches, the head will fall. That's when the knockout punch comes.

At the age of ten, I was taking a lot of body blows.

I discovered that my father was not really my father. That the person I thought was my father had rejected me.

One Saturday afternoon, while Crystal was away, I came out of my room and found Mom in the kitchen, peeling potatoes for dinner. I was feeling down for being left out again and desperately needed my mother's comfort.

"I don't have a father, Mom." I barely choked out the words.

Mom looked up from her peeling. "Stop being weak," she said coldly. "You're using that as a crutch to lean on. I don't want to hear about it, so quit whining. I don't have time for this. You have to be strong."

I left the room more despondent than before. I needed to be comforted, hugged, and caressed. Instead, my mother blew me off. She had no emotional reservoir to tap into. She was empty and had nothing to give me. I felt unwanted, unloved, and unprotected.

I was hitting continuously on all three of these chords that were leading me to a dark place. When you're unwanted, that's bad enough. When you're unloved, that's bad enough. But when you're unprotected, the next step is surrender.

I learned that things were best when I didn't make waves. I did my best to be invisible. I thought, *If I'm invisible, then nobody can get mad at me. If I'm invisible, I won't get a whupping.*

There were moments when Mom thrashed me pretty good if I did something to tick her off, so I became the quietest kid you could imagine. Whatever Mom wanted or demanded of me, I did without complaint. I complied to survive—emotionally and physically. I didn't want to get another spanking or tongue-lashing for doing something wrong.

Most of the time I flew under the radar. But one evening I made a huge mistake.

It happened when I put on my pajamas after dinner and a bath. I couldn't help but notice that my pajamas had holes in them. I'm talking holes in the knees, holes in the seat of my bottoms, and holes in the arms. Holes everywhere.

It was late winter, and I was cold. I needed new pajamas.

I walked down the stairs to the kitchen, where Mom was cleaning up.

"Mom, my pajamas have holes," I told her. I wanted her to know—and care—that my PJs were worn out and I needed a new pair.

I don't know what she had gone through that day—if she got a notice that the utilities were going to be turned off or if there was an unexpected car repair—but she looked at me with fury in her eyes.

"You tore them on purpose! You just want some attention!"

"No, Mom! It's cold upstairs."

"Your pajamas have holes?" she asked rhetorically. "Well, maybe we should put some more holes in them. Then you'll know what a pair of pajamas with a lot of holes is really like."

Following that preamble, Mom went crazy. Her hands were all over me, grabbing my pajamas and ripping them to shreds like a wolf attacking a lamb. In the process, her long, lacquered fingernails scratched up my body as remnants of torn flannel fell to the floor. Resistance was futile. Within a minute, I stood before her buck naked with a pair of ripped-up pajamas at my feet.

I gathered up my tattered clothes and shuffled off to my bedroom, where I banged my head against the wall behind my bed and thought, *You know what? I'm never going to talk again. I'm never going to tell anybody I need a new anything. I'm never going to let anyone know I'm weak and hurting.*

I cried myself to sleep that night, but in my last waking moment, I formed a plan in my mind. The next time I was home alone, I would kill myself.

I was tired of being rejected, dismayed, mortified to speak in class, yelled at for wetting my bed, and deeply hurt by schoolyard taunts.

I saw a way out of my misery.

If Mom could fire a gun, then I could too.

•   •   •

The following day, a Saturday, my stepfather picked Crystal up in the morning. They were off to Canton to see relatives.

At lunchtime, Mom asked me if I wanted to go into the city with her and Aunt Ann. There wasn't anything more boring in the world than shopping, so I asked if I could stay home. Mom said yes.

Once they left, I knew this was my chance to act on my plan. For most of the afternoon, I was in the basement watching cartoons on TV and thinking about how I would soon put myself out of my misery.

I knew that sooner or later Mom and Aunt Ann would be back from their shopping excursion. If I was going to do this, then the time was now.

I walked up the stairs to Mom's bedroom and sat on her bed next to the nightstand. I reached for the drawer and opened it. There it was—the shiny nickel-plated snub-nosed revolver and a small box of bullets.

I opened up the box first and examined the ammunition. The bullets had shiny gold casings and were tipped with a copper-looking head.

I took one bullet out of the box and held it up. I was amazed that such a small cartridge could do so much destruction to the human body. I bit on the end of the bullet—not hard because I didn't want it to explode. I just wanted to feel the tip. I was surprised that my teeth could sink into the material. The bullet tip was that malleable. I saw teeth marks.

I set the cartridge back in the box and looked at the revolver. The handle was tan, and the barrel looked to be about two or three inches long. I had never picked up the handgun before, so when I reached for it, I was surprised that such a small gun felt so heavy in my hand.

I held up the gun and peered at the tips of the bullets in the six chambers in the cylinder. I breathed a sigh of relief. I wouldn't have to load the gun to end my life.

Because that's what I had decided to do. I wasn't turning back. In just a moment, I was going to point the gun at my temple and end it all.

I contemplated what would happen when the gun fired. Sure, the explosion would hurt, but only for a fleeting moment. After that, I would be free—free from kids at school who made fun of me, free from the bullies in the schoolyard, and free from my wretched existence.

I studied the snub-nosed revolver one more time.

Did I really want to do this?

The answer was yes.

I stepped away from the bed and positioned myself next to the wall. I had seen cop shows and gangster movies, so when I blew my brains out, I wanted all the blood and gore to splatter against the wall. *Then they'll find out how bad things were for me*, I thought.

I held the gun in my right hand and raised it to my head. I pressed the barrel against my temple.

Without any hesitation, I pulled the trigger.

• • •

I was still here.

The trigger didn't budge when I pressed it.

I looked into the barrel of the revolver. I saw darkness, a void I had been willing to step into an instant earlier. I was prepared to enter the great unknown—whatever death was— but nothing happened.

My eyes darted around Mom's bedroom. Yes, I was still here. Everything was the same, which meant I was still a stutterer, still unloved, still a laughingstock at school.

I repositioned myself next to the wall. The handgun still felt cold in my hand. I raised it to my right temple a second time, clenched my teeth, and squeezed again. The trigger moved a little bit, but nothing happened.

Now what do I do?

I didn't have a clue. I hadn't thought this far ahead. I was supposed to be dead.

I tried pressing the trigger three or four more times, each time expecting an explosion that would blow my brains out, but nothing transpired.

I sat down on Mom's bed and set the gun on the bedspread. A solitary thought filled my mind: *I'm so pitiful that I can't even kill myself.*

I stared at the gun. *Can't I do anything right?* I picked up the snub-nosed revolver and put it to my temple one more time, but it wouldn't fire.

The gun must be broken.

At ten years old, I didn't know there was a safety on the gun or that I had to push a button to free the safety. I wasn't mechanically inclined, and no one had showed me how to operate a handgun. I figured instead that the gun was defective and left it at that.

Deep, deep down, I wasn't disappointed. I mean, I didn't *want* to die. Who really does? It's just that I didn't see a reason to keep living.

I looked at the gun one last time and shrugged my shoulders. I returned the deadly weapon to Mom's nightstand, exactly as I had found it.

I fell back on Mom's bed and contemplated what else I could do to kill myself. Maybe I could step in front of a train. The Erie Railroad line wasn't too far away, but the thought of a powerful locomotive crunching every bone in my body gave me pause. I didn't think I could step in front of a moving train.

Then I remembered seeing the James Bond movie *Goldfinger,* where 007 flung his assailant into a bathtub filled with water and tossed an electric heater in behind him, causing the man to sizzle and smoke in an agonizing death. I didn't want to drop an electric radio into my bathtub and kill myself that way either.

What about swallowing rat poison? There were always big rodents snooping around our house as well as Grannie's, so I knew about rat poison. Then I recalled my uncles describing in grisly detail what really happened when rats ate the poison. They didn't stop breathing, my uncles chortled. What happened was that the rats became really thirsty and began bleeding internally until their guts practically exploded. I imagined taking a gulp of rat poison and experiencing an explosion in my abdomen so that my insides would become my outsides. The thought of a slow, agonizing death sounded horrific to me. A bullet would be better, right?

But I had already tried that method and failed.

When Mom and Aunt Ann came home, they found me on the living room couch, reading one of my Childcraft encyclopedias. I was hoping there would be something in one of the volumes about an easy way to commit suicide, but I wasn't having any luck.

"You hungry, Skeezix?" Mom set her packages down on a chest of drawers near the front door.

My face brightened. "What's for dinner?"

"Special treat. I got a fryer I can cut up. How about some fried chicken?"

We didn't eat like that every night. "With fried potatoes?"

"Of course! I know they're your favorite."

I watched as Mom and Aunt Ann got things squared away in the kitchen. I maintained a happy face, but inside, my guts were churning.

I was a mixed-up kid who had just tried to commit suicide. I felt like I had this horrible secret that I couldn't share with anyone. Even though I tried to be cheerful, I ate dinner in silence, allowing Mom and Aunt Ann to talk about adult stuff that I wasn't interested in. I kept thinking, *If they only knew how close I came to killing myself today* ...

But I couldn't say anything. Not only would they not understand, I knew Mom would get mad at me. I hadn't forgotten the previous night, when she'd torn my ratty pajamas to shreds in a fit of rage.

We watched a little TV after dinner and then I went to bed. I banged my head against the wall like I normally did, and then I fell asleep.

In the morning, Mom had to change the sheets. I had wet them again.

Nothing had changed, and I had no hope that anything would get better in my life. There was nothing but discouragement and despondency for me.

I didn't have the love I needed, the direction I required, the teaching I yearned for, or the innocence I longed for. I had been abused by people who were supposed to protect me, had been teased heartlessly by other kids, and was a failure in trying to kill myself.

And it was here, at my lowest point, that hope finally found me.

6

_

EXODUS

At least I was out of the basement.

For fifth grade, I was allowed to rejoin my regular class. My school always started the year by mainstreaming all students. Then teachers would rank them: the outstanding kids, the average kids, and the special-needs kids, who were sent to the basement. I didn't want to go back to the school basement, so I paid attention in class.

I still did everything I could *not* to talk, however. I sat on my hands and hoped and wished and prayed the teacher wouldn't call on me. My fifth-grade teacher was a young white woman in her late twenties, and she reminded me of Cruella de Vil from Disney's *101 Dalmatians*. She was not a good teacher. She was mean. She never smiled. She always spoke down to the students and copped an attitude.

I did my best to keep my head down and steer clear of her. And for the most part, I lucked out. Cruella left me alone, which was remarkable since she had surely seen me struggle to string several words together without stammering.

Four or five days after I tried to kill myself—sometime in March 1974—I was working on some math problems with the rest of my class. My teacher walked the aisles, looking over our shoulders. She stopped at my desk, which sent a shudder through my body. I didn't like to be singled out.

She discreetly leaned over. "Come see me at the end of school," she whispered.

Fear washed over me. *What have I done now? Is she going to send me back to the basement?*

My teacher continued making her rounds. I felt like I was twisting in the wind.

I could barely concentrate on my schoolwork the rest of the day. As I watched the clock tick ever so slowly, the final bell rang at 2:40.

My classmates sprinted for the door while I trudged to Cruella's desk at the front of the classroom.

"Do you know Mrs. Spears?" she asked.

The name sounded familiar. "Isn't sh-sh-she a tea . . . teacher?"

"You're right. Mrs. Spears teaches sixth grade. She would like to see you."

"How c-c-c-come?" I couldn't imagine why a schoolteacher would want to see me unless I was in some sort of trouble.

"I'm not sure. You'll have to ask her. You'll find her in Room Fourteen."

I found out years later that Mrs. Spears had heard about me in the teachers' lounge. Another teacher had told her, "Ronaldo's a nice young man. He's not a disrespectful kid. He just stutters a lot. He's afraid to talk to anyone. He seems to be in a low place and has no confidence in himself."

Mrs. Spears didn't have to teach in the inner city, but she wanted to. She was a Christian woman and saw our school as a mission field. She had a heart for the most troubled kids, and I certainly fit in that category.

I gathered my belongings and walked to Mrs. Spears's room. I found her sitting behind her desk, grading papers. She was a white woman with graying hair. She wasn't as old as Grannie, but she wasn't my mother's age either. She appeared nice, though.

"Hello, Ronaldo. I'm glad you came today. Have a seat, young man." Mrs. Spears spoke slowly, drawing out each syllable. There was a twang to her voice. She was obviously from the South and had an accent that I didn't hear very often in Cleveland. Her Southern accent wasn't heavy, though. I'd call it Kentucky sweet— kind of like grits and honey.

I slid into a seat in the row nearest Mrs. Spears's desk. She folded her hands and looked right into my eyes. "Would you like to speak better? Would you like to speak well?"

I shrugged in a way that signaled *yes*. I didn't want to say anything and hear myself stutter. That wouldn't make a very good first impression.

"Good," she said, "because I'm willing to help you. We'll start *real* slow."

I remained mute and wondered what would happen next.

"Let's begin with some breathing exercises. I want you to breathe in and out, just like I'm going to do."

Mrs. Spears drew in air through her nose and exhaled through her mouth. I did the same. She repeated this exercise several times.

"Good. Now I want you to place one hand on your stomach and one hand on your chest." Mrs. Spears showed me where to place my hands. "When you breathe in and out, I want you to feel your diaphragm move. Your diaphragm separates your chest from the abdomen and is the main muscle for respiration."

We did this exercise several times as well. "Now I want you to practice making these sounds with me. Are you ready?"

I nodded.

"Lee-lee, la-la, lo-lo. Can you say that? Lee-lee, la-la, lo-lo."

The moment of truth. I actually had to say something.

"Lee . . . lee . . . la . . . la . . ."

Not a bad start, but I had forgotten the last one.

Mrs. Spears filled in the blank. "Lo-lo."

"Lo . . . lo . . ." I repeated.

"Let's try it again: Lee-lee, la-la, lo-lo."

The second time I said it a little faster: "Lee-lee . . . la-la . . . lo-lo . . ."

"Again."

"Lee-lee, la-la, lo-lo."

"You're getting it. Again."

"Lee-lee, la-la, lo-lo."

"It's okay to hold the *L* until you feel comfortable."

"Lee-lee, la-la, lo-lo."

She must have asked me to say that phrase twenty times or more. I didn't understand this at ten years old, but what Mrs. Spears was doing was getting me to relax my tongue and my mouth. Repeating these short syllables that combined an initial *L* sound with a single vowel allowed me to gain confidence while my tongue learned to form the sounds in my mouth.

"Lee-lee, la-la, lo-lo."

"Lee-lee, la-la, lo-lo."

I was starting to get into a rhythm. She had me repeat the phrase another twenty times, each time a bit faster and a bit clearer. Even though I wasn't stuttering, I still felt like I had a long way to go before it felt natural.

When my stuttering was at its worst, it felt like I had no control over what came out of my mouth. My whole body felt discombobulated. When I stuttered and stammered, unable to finish a sentence, I felt like an overloaded washing machine that shut down during the spin cycle because too much clothing had bunched up on one side of the drum.

Stuttering came with the heart-wrenching realization that I couldn't express what I wanted to say. Trying hard *not* to stammer only made things worse because the more muscular exertion I applied, the more my words stuck in my throat. If I started to sound out a word, I couldn't get past the first or second syllable no matter how hard I tried. When that happened—say in a classroom of kids—blood rushed to my cheeks. I felt like my ears were burning. Sometimes my stuttering got so bad that I would shake like I was having convulsions. I hated the feeling of hopelessness and helplessness swelling inside me until I felt like there was nothing more I could do.

But here I was with Mrs. Spears, gaining confidence with the simple cadence of *Lee-lee, la-la, lo-lo.*

"You're doing just fine," she said. We had practiced for around forty-five minutes. "Can you come back tomorrow?"

I nodded. But I wasn't going to press my luck by saying "Sure."

Those *S* sounds had always given me trouble.

•   •   •

For the first time I could ever remember, I *wanted* to go to school when I ate my bowl of cereal the following morning. I didn't want to wait all day to see Mrs. Spears, but that was the deal.

She was at her desk when I arrived shortly after the final bell. The last of her students were leaving the classroom for the day.

Mrs. Spears was calm and loving. She had big eyes and a beautiful smile. "Anything worth doing in life is worth doing poorly at first until you get better," she told me.

That made sense to me.

"Remember when you couldn't tie your shoes? You couldn't do that well at first. But what happened? You kept trying, and before you knew it, you could tie your shoes with your eyes closed."

I nodded.

"Do you like to ride a bike?"

I nodded again.

"Remember when you would ride your bicycle and fall and crash? But you got up, and now you can ride that bike any way you want. I bet you can do wheelies and really pop it. Learning how to speak better is the same thing. It takes some time, but you'll get it. Why? Because you *want* to get it. So let's get started today with our breathing exercises again."

After our warm-up, we moved smoothly into *Lee-lee, la-la, lo-lo*.

"Pay attention to the way you enunciate the vowel sounds— *lee* . . . then *la* . . . then *lo* . . ."

After working on that a few times, she introduced a new phrase to work on: *At dawn the don went down.*

Mrs. Spears had me overemphasize the vowel sounds so I could learn to breathe as I spoke *dawn*, *don*, and *down*.

"At dawn the don went down."

"At dawn the don went down."

"At dawn the don went down."

"See? You are actually feeling the words," she said. "You want your body to *feel* the sound and know the rhythm of every word you speak. Let's try another one: *Are our oars here?*"

This was tougher. I tripped over *are our* and mangled those two short words. But Mrs. Spears patiently helped me through by having me work on *are our* and then *oars here* until I could say it all together.

"Are our oars here?"

"Again."

"Are our oars here?"

Mrs. Spears explained that we were working on my end consonants with this phrase, which I was having trouble with.

Before, I had been filled with nervous tension whenever I tried to speak. My words got stuck in my throat and created a stutter. But when Mrs. Spears showed me how to focus on the end consonants, speaking became like playing a percussion instrument, like hitting a drum or a cymbal. End consonants gave me a cadence and a rhythm and time to collect myself before I went to the next word—time to pause.

End vowels, on the other hand, were different. They were like stringed instruments—like a violin. Those needed to be elongated.

Mrs. Spears's pet phrases became my mantra:

"Lee-lee, la-la, lo-lo."

"At dawn the don went down."

"Are our oars here?"

With each success, speaking out loud was becoming smoother. Mrs. Spears likened my success to hitting a baseball properly. "The more you try to swing hard or overswing, the better chance you'll have to strike out," she explained. "But once you relax your body and let your legs and arms swing through the ball, the more likely you'll connect—and connect with power. It's the same way with talking. Be alert to your vowels and end consonants, and feel like you're getting into a rhythm so that you can let it go and let it flow."

I soaked up everything Mrs. Spears said like a sponge.

We continued to meet every day after school for a half hour to forty-five minutes. After a week together, she wanted to work on the *S* sound.

*S*s had been my downfall for as long as I could remember. I'd get s-s-s-stuck on the *S* sound and give up. Then I couldn't say anything.

"Relax your jaw and say, 'The sea.'"

I repeated that simple phrase once, twice, and then a dozen times.

"Good. You're relaxing your muscles. Now I want you to close your eyes."

Sitting in front of her desk, I did as she asked.

"Imagine you're sitting in a warm bath. Now you're done and putting on your favorite jammies. You're feeling warm and relaxed. Now you're sitting on your favorite couch, curled up with a good book. You're comfortable."

Mrs. Spears's syrupy words were nearly hypnotic. I felt my shoulders drop immediately. Up until then, my shoulder muscles had been tight, as well as my neck.

"You feel the tension loosening up in your shoulders?" she asked.

"Yes."

"Good. Allow your neck to relax, and then your jaw. They're all connected. Think of the ocean. Think of the water. Just see it."

My eyes remained closed as Mrs. Spears continued.

"*The sea.* Just say the words and relax."

"The sea . . . the sea . . . the sea . . ."

Next came a tongue twister that threatened to destroy all my progress: *The seething sea ceaseth and thus the seething sea sufficeth us.*

I gulped. This sounded impossible. But over the course of the next half hour, Mrs. Spears broke each word down until I was able to say the sentence haltingly.

"You're doing well," she said. "Focus and finish. You can do this."

She was right. Eventually, I could successfully say *The seething sea ceaseth and thus the seething sea sufficeth us.*

Next, we went to the *P*s, which had a way of lassoing me as well.

"Repeat after me: 'Proper preparation prevents poor performance,'" she said. "Speak slowly and overemphasize the consonant sounds."

"Proper preparation prevents poor performance."

"Proper preparation prevents poor performance."

"Proper preparation prevents poor performance."

We didn't stop there. Over the next month, I also became best friends with Sally, who sold seashells by the seashore; Peter Piper, who picked a peck of pickled peppers; and Susie, who was sitting in a shoeshine shop.

I repeated these short sayings so often that I memorized them. Instead of falling asleep banging my head against the wall,

I'd softly repeat these phrases. Now they were rolling off my tongue instead of getting me all knotted up.

• • •

After a month or so, I was doing much better, and I noticed that Mrs. Spears was pleased, which made me feel even better about myself.

The next step was having conversations.

"Remember, you're not in a race," she said. "You don't have to be in a hurry. You don't have to beat somebody to the finish line. These are your words. It's your voice. You can be in control. You want to take your time. There's no rush."

"Right, Mrs. Spears."

One afternoon, Mrs. Spears told me, "Ronaldo, I believe God has tremendous plans for you. I'm honored that He's allowed me to partner with you and work with you."

"Thank you, Mrs. Spears."

"To make our lesson more interesting, I want you to read into a tape recorder."

I had never spoken into a tape recorder, so consequently, I'd never heard myself speak. This being the early 1970s, tape recorders were still relatively uncommon. I wasn't sure what to think, so I didn't say anything.

"What do you say we give it a try?" Mrs. Spears said. "It can't hurt, right?"

There was such encouragement in her words. "Okay," I managed.

Mrs. Spears stepped over to a small table with wheels next to her desk. On top of the table was a big reel-to-reel tape recorder with a gigantic microphone.

She had me read a Dr. Seuss book, and then we listened to the playback.

My voice sounded high-pitched and raspy. "I sound like that?"

"You have a wonderful voice for someone your age," Mrs. Sears said.

And then Mrs. Spears said something that would change my life. "Did you know you're in the Bible? I can show you."

"I'm in the Bible?"

"Yes, you are, young man."

I knew what the Bible was, but we weren't a churchgoing family. I could remember going to church a few times, like at Christmas or Easter, but my knowledge of religion came from watching *The Ten Commandments* and *Ben-Hur* on TV. I couldn't imagine being in a big, important book like the Bible, so I was curious what Mrs. Spears meant.

"Where am I in the Bible?"

Mrs. Spears patiently reached for a thick, leather-bound volume on her desk. I'd noticed that big book before. Sometimes she was reading it when I walked into her classroom.

"I'm going to turn to the book of Jeremiah, the first chapter, starting in verse four. Can you read what it says to me?"

I hoped there weren't going to be any big words or words I had never seen before. The Bible was mysterious to me.

I didn't say a word while Mrs. Spears turned the Bible around and pointed to a place on the left page. "Start here," she said.

I found the spot and started reading:

Then the word of the LORD came unto me, saying,
Before I formed thee in the belly I knew thee . . . and I
ordained thee a prophet unto the nations.

JEREMIAH 1:4-5

"See?" Mrs. Spears said. "God himself planned your birth. You're no accident or mistake."

What an earth-shattering thing to hear at that exact moment in time. It felt as though God was telling me, *You were not a mistake. You weren't the happenstance meeting of two strangers in the dark. You weren't just some thing that happened to be born.*

God was telling me I was truly special. I had never thought of myself in that manner. In fact, I was so down on life in general and myself in particular that I had been ready to end it just a month or so earlier.

"Can you continue reading?" she asked.

I found my spot again. The words came out haltingly, but I managed:

> Then said I, Ah, Lord GOD! behold, I cannot speak:
> for I am a child. But the LORD said unto me, Say not, I
> am a child: for thou shalt go to all that I shall send thee,
> and whatsoever I command thee thou shalt speak. Be not
> afraid of their faces: for I am with thee to deliver thee,
> saith the LORD. Then the LORD put forth his hand, and
> touched my mouth. And the LORD said unto me, Behold,
> I have put my words in thy mouth. See, I have this day
> set thee over the nations and over the kingdoms, to root
> out, and to pull down, and to destroy, and to throw
> down, to build, and to plant.
>
> JEREMIAH 1:6-10

Even though I stammered a couple of times, I was nearly at a loss for words when I finished reading these verses. Tears formed, which I wiped away with the back of my hand. For the first time, I felt *good* about myself. I felt *good* about who I was. I felt *good* that I wasn't a mistake or an unwanted child.

"God planted you in your mother's womb for a specific purpose," Mrs. Spears said. "You have a destiny to fulfill. You have something that He wants you to do."

Hearing those words really filled my sails. Wow! What an earth-shattering, paradigm-shifting, upside-down-turning perspective. God Himself had planned my birth for a divine purpose! I didn't know what that purpose was, but reading this section of Scripture opened my ears to listen.

The next time we met, Mrs. Spears asked me, "Did you know that Moses was a stutterer?"

"He was?" I couldn't believe there'd be a stutterer in such a holy book as the Bible. When I watched *The Ten Commandments* on TV, Moses—played by Charlton Heston—didn't stutter. I would have picked up on that.

"Let's read about him," said my teacher.

She took me to the book of Exodus, where we worked our way through the story of Moses. After reading about how a Hebrew mother had hid her baby boy in a basket and set it on the Nile River (since Pharaoh had ordered that all Hebrew boys be killed), I was fascinated to learn that Moses grew up in Pharaoh's palace. Then, as a young man, Moses learned who he really was. One day, he killed an Egyptian slave master beating a Hebrew because of the injustice being committed. Fearing for *his* life, Moses fled Egypt for Midian, where he married Zipporah and tended flocks for forty years.

Then his story really got interesting. When Moses met the angel of the Lord in the burning bush, God told him that he was going to be the instrument to lead the Hebrew nation out of Egypt and to the Promised Land. That meant confronting Pharaoh, and the person to do that, God told Moses, was him. Moses was scared stiff and responded, "O my LORD, I am not eloquent, neither heretofore nor since thou hast spoken unto thy servant: but I am slow of speech, and of a slow tongue" (Exodus 4:10, KJV).

Modern translations render the last sentence as "I get tongue-tied, and my words get tangled" (NLT) or "I stutter and stammer"

(MSG). Back then, when I was ten years old, I knew why Mrs. Spears wanted me to read that passage. "See? Moses was a stutterer, just like you were," she said.

Reading how Moses returned to Egypt and led the oppressed Hebrew people out of bondage resonated with my imagination. Moses became everything to me. I identified with him. He was my hero! There were so many things about him that I fell in love with, and I wanted to emulate Moses in any way possible.

I read more about him in one of my Childcraft volumes. Then I remembered I had a dashiki in the closet. I started wearing my dashiki and told my mother and sister, "Call me Moses. I'm Moses now."

Mom folded her arms. "You're off your rocker, boy!" she announced with a smirk.

Crystal wasn't as generous. "Why are you acting so stupid?"

I found a big stick in the neighborhood, so now I had a staff, just like the Hebrew leader. With my dashiki and my stick, I loved pretending I was Moses.

Mrs. Spears had me read Bible stories from Genesis, like the story of Joseph and how he was sold into slavery by his brothers and ended up rescuing his family from famine. The story of Noah and the Flood. Abraham being asked by God to sacrifice his only son, Isaac, only to be held back by the angel of the Lord at the last possible moment.

I identified with Isaac. He wasn't much older than me, but he thought he was going to die—just like I did. I wondered what he thought about his close call with death. I loved learning about these wonderful characters and how this wonderful God would step in at just the right time to save them.

I felt at that moment that Mrs. Spears was brought to me at my lowest point to be my Jethro. Jethro, Moses's father-in-law, was a great encourager and counselor, and so was Mrs. Spears. I had always had an affinity for older white women because of my grandmother, and Mrs. Spears fit right into that mold. I had a natural sense of safety with her, so I was open to her instruction.

"The person at the top of the mountain did not fall there," she said. "He had to climb there, and so do you."

Mrs. Spears stepped away from her desk and came to where I was seated in one of her students' desks.

"Do you know that you could help your whole family?"

Immediately I thought about Mom and Grannie and Big Daddy and my aunts and uncles. That interested me right away. "But how can I help my entire family?" I didn't see how it was possible.

"Education can change your whole family."

"Really?"

"Sure. You know why education is so important?" she asked.

I knew the answer to that question. Mom had certain pillars she believed in, and education was at the center. I remembered how she always used to say, "Empty wagons make the most noise," meaning the loudest person in the room was typically the one with nothing in his head.

Mrs. Spears broke my reverie. "Because education makes you smart," she said. "Well, it's more than that. You see, an education is one of the few things in life that once you get it, they can never take it back from you. They can take your house, they can take your car, they can take your clothing, they can take your jewelry, and they can take your land. But once you have an education, it's all yours for the rest of your life."

Mom had said the same thing, so she and Mrs. Spears were on the same page.

"Ronaldo, people are going to listen to you. Just you wait and see. All you need is a good education."

That was good to hear. I didn't want to grow up and become an empty wagon.

• • •

One of my best friends in fifth grade was Kevin Anderson.

He sat in the desk in front of me because the class sat alphabetically . . . Anderson, Archer, Bailey, etc. Kevin was one of my best friends at a time when I didn't have many.

Perhaps Kevin and I got along because he wasn't a popular kid either. He had cerebral palsy, a condition that affected his ability to control the muscles of his body. This meant his arms and legs could flutter and move suddenly. Kevin had problems with balance and coordination.

Sometimes when he sat in his chair, his left leg would protrude into the aisle because he couldn't control where it went. He wore braces on his legs to help him walk better.

One day, just before the end of the fifth-grade school year and after three months of steady after-school help from Mrs. Spears, my teacher Cruella was walking around the classroom, giving us a spelling test. When she passed my desk, she looked down at her list to announce the next word.

That's when she tripped over Kevin's outstretched leg. She was only just able to catch her balance.

Once Cruella collected herself, she lit into Kevin. She grabbed the ruler on his desk and started beating him with it.

"You tried to trip me!" she shrieked.

Whack! Whack!

I couldn't believe I was witnessing this injustice. She knew that Kevin had cerebral palsy and couldn't control his extremities.

I stood up—and grabbed her hand! "That's not true, ma'am," I pleaded. "He can't control where his leg goes, so you shouldn't be beating him. That's unfair."

Cruella regarded me with a look of shock on her face. She twisted her hand free from my grasp and straightened her frazzled hair.

"Go to the principal's office right now!"

"Why?"

"Because I said so!"

"Yes, ma'am."

All eyes watched me depart the classroom. This was a first for me, being sent to the principal. And then it hit me—I hadn't stammered at all. My stutter was gone! I had spoken several complete sentences out loud and in public before my peers. And I had spoken flawlessly while under pressure! Everything flowed out of my mouth naturally, just as Mrs. Spears had said it would. I had spoken fluently, powerfully, and with conviction. This was also the first moment in my life when I stood up for something.

As I walked to the principal's office, I thought about what I could do when I got older. I determined that I wanted to speak up for those who were disadvantaged and couldn't speak up for themselves.

That sounded like a worthy vocation—speaking out for the underdog.

I certainly knew what being an underdog was like.

PART 2

TURN

7

THE SOCIAL NETWORK

With my stepfather out of the house, I struggled to figure out what was going on. As nice as Mrs. Spears was to me, I had no social network to draw upon for emotional support. I had no church, no counselors, and no psychiatrists. I had to figure things out for myself, which means I wasn't figuring things out.

Many questions still rattled around in my mind, usually along the lines of *What's going to happen? Are we going to have to move? Is my stepfather coming back? What's going to happen if he does come back?*

Whenever I felt Mom was in a good enough mood, I'd ask her my questions. But then her resentment would flare to the surface.

"Shut up and be thankful you have food on the table!" she would reply sharply. "You have clothes to wear. You have a roof over your head. I don't have time for these questions. Do you know how hard it is to keep this house together?"

Whenever Mom snapped at me like that, I did my best to keep my head down and stay clear of her. I learned quickly that when she was short-tempered or in a bad mood, that would be a good time to disappear and get lost in my Childcraft encyclopedias.

Sometimes I'd lie on my bed and think about my sister returning from a shopping spree with the man I had once thought was my father. She would step inside the front door with an armload of presents—toys, clothing, and sweet treats. Her favorite candy was Tootsie Pops. She'd lick the hard candy coating until she reached the simple, delicious, chewy Tootsie Roll center. Would she ever share her stash with me? Not a chance.

When I'd plead my case with Mom, asking her to tell Crystal to share with me, my mother would remain mute. I found out years later that my mother wanted to maintain good relations with my stepfather's family because her mother-in-law was sending money to keep the mortgage paid. Mom didn't want to do anything to upset his side of the family. She saw Crystal as a financial godsend since it was on her account that Mom was getting the mortgage money. I, on the other hand, was a burden—another mouth to feed. That changed, ever so slightly, when my mother was able to get on ADC—Aid to Dependent Children, a federal program. Then she needed me because I was a dependent she could claim.

•   •   •

Mom was still going out two or three nights a week.

I got used to watching her primp her hair and touch up her makeup before leaving the house and placing us in the care of Aunt Ann for the evening. I still thought Mom was the most beautiful thing in the world, even though she wasn't the motherly type who smothered me with kisses and baked fresh chocolate chip cookies when I got home from school. But she was the only parent I had.

At some level, I knew she had my best interests at heart. I say that because she constantly talked about the importance of getting a good education and complimented me whenever she saw my nose in a book. She was on me to do my homework and checked my math exercises and test results.

Mom was aware of how the cycle of poverty cast a pall over our poor, working-class neighborhood. The best way to break out of that cycle was to get an education or an athletic scholarship, even though she didn't believe the latter could happen with me since I had been a sickly kid and didn't seem to be a natural athlete. She pinned her hopes on my becoming educated, which sounds clichéd, but this was bound to be difficult to pull off since I attended an inner-city school, where academic standards were reduced to the lowest common denominator.

Despite Mom's care in other ways, she didn't know how much her going out destabilized our family. Something wasn't right, a little bit off, and I could see it in the knowing glances Mom and Aunt Ann exchanged each time my well-coifed mother reached the front door and said her goodbyes. It was bad enough that Mom was going out, but soon she started entertaining "boyfriends" at our place.

The first few times she brought strange men into our home, it was after bedtime. I remember hearing muffled voices at the front door followed by two adults climbing the wooden staircase to the master bedroom on the second floor.

I was starting to put the pieces together: there was something sexual going on between Mom and these "boyfriends" in her company. This was confirmed one night when I tiptoed out of my bedroom and looked through the keyhole. I couldn't see much, but I saw enough to understand they weren't playing checkers.

The following evening, a conversation I overheard between Mom and Aunt Ann made more sense.

"Make sure you get paid first."

"Yeah, yeah. I know."

"Men will cheat you, if they can."

"Yeah, yeah."

After a while, my mother didn't wait until a late hour to bring home boyfriends. I'd be down in the basement watching TV shows like *Fat Albert and the Cosby Kids* or *Sanford and Son* and hear the front door open. Voices were muted. Then I'd hear the footsteps going up the stairs to her bedroom.

It was hard to wrap my mind around what Mom was doing. I mean, I knew *what* they were doing, but the *why* escaped me. In the fifth grade I didn't have a good concept of what sex between strangers really constituted—that sex could be a transaction between a man and a woman instead of a loving act.

•   •   •

I'll never forget the first Christmas without my stepfather. Even though we were struggling to get by, Mom decorated the house for Christmas like we were in a German home. As in past years, she played the "Nutcracker Suite" on the hi-fi and hung mistletoe. Christmas, like I said, was a festive time and a big deal to Mom. This holiday season, however, there was just a handful of small gifts under the tree as compared to past years, when there had been a mountain of presents waiting to be unwrapped.

One night after dinner, we were clearing the plates when Mom lit into me after I asked her if I was going to get a bike for Christmas.

"Do you want Christmas? Do you want presents and toys?" she demanded. "Then call Mr. Thomas and tell him what a great guy he is!"

I wished I hadn't asked. I didn't know who Mr. Thomas was. I figured he was one of Mom's "boyfriends."

"But Mom—"

"You want Christmas, don't you?"

"Well, yeah."

Mom turned on her heels and found a little black book next to the phone. Her fingers did the walking, and then she found the name she was looking for.

A few strokes of the rotary phone, and then she waved me over to take the handset.

"What should I say?" I whispered.

"Just thank him for being your mother's friend."

I gulped, and then I heard a man's deep voice say, "Hello."

"Oh, hi. Is this Mr. Thomas?"

"Yes. And whom do I have the pleasure of speaking with today?"

"This is Ronaldo Archer. Thank you so much for being Mom's friend. And thank you for all the things you give us."

"You're welcome, young man."

"I better go now. Goodbye."

And I hung up.

My mother beamed. "See, that wasn't so difficult."

"Did I do okay?"

"You did just fine. He's got money. You'll see."

There was an awkward pause. I didn't know what to say, but Mom gave me a window into her thinking. Everything in her life was about money—making it, saving it, and stretching it. I saw how she would go to farmers markets and buy lots of vegetables and make chili and spaghetti sauces—stick-to-your-ribs meals that would last. Cheese casseroles were served regularly. Nothing was wasted; leftovers were a staple.

I don't blame her for thinking that way. She didn't have much money to work with, so saving a few dollars any way she could became really important. No matter how little she had, she told me that she always put away a bit of money.

"It's like this," she said one day. "You have three ears of corn. One ear of corn you eat to survive. The second ear of corn you reinvest in the ground to produce more corn. And the third ear you put away in case there is a famine. You try to live your life on one ear of corn while making the other two ears work for you."

That was her mindset, which was very astute. When she pocketed some cash, she was always thinking about how much we could live on and how much she should save for a rainy day.

I remember talking to her once when I knew her birthday was coming up. Mom had always showered me with gifts on my birthday, so I wanted to do the same for her. I had a piggy bank filled with coins and dollar bills given to me by Big Daddy and Grannie.

"What would you like for your birthday?" I asked.

Mom was matter of fact. "Don't buy me perfume. Don't buy me clothing. Don't buy me anything. Always give me money."

"Why?"

"Because money is always the right size and the right color and never goes out of style."

I was getting the idea why Mom did what she did in the evenings—it was for the money. There was an evolution of understanding for me; I was slowly but surely making sense of the world around me. At the same time, an undercurrent of shame flowed like a river, threatening our family's already-weak foundation.

I wish there were more moments when Mom showed me love and compassion, but her priority was food, clothing, and a home. The basics were a challenge and consumed her. She told me she had to drop out of high school because I came along, which always made me feel guilty—as if I was the reason we were in this tough spot.

There's no doubt that my mom was a good provider. I was never without food or clothing. Something drove her. She reminded me of Scarlett O'Hara in *Gone with the Wind*. In the movie, the crop has dried up during a famine. There is a scene at the end where Scarlett is standing in the devastated garden of her family's plantation that was ruined by the Union army during the Civil War. Scarlett shakes her fist at the heavens and declares, "As God is my witness, they're not going to lick me . . . as God is my witness, I'll never be hungry again."

Mom told me stories about how she had gone hungry as a child, when potato soup was all they had. "That's how we lived," she said, her eyes glistening from the memory. "That's how we survived. My brothers stole food so we'd have something to eat. I never want to be that desperate. I'm doing everything I can so we can have a home to live in and enough to eat."

I didn't doubt that my mother was a good provider. The problem is that I didn't have her heart during much of my childhood. She didn't know how to emotionally connect or communicate in a loving manner. The way she showed love was by providing for me and my sister.

•   •   •

One time I noticed that Mom had a little black-and-white TV on the chest of drawers in her bedroom.

"Where did you get that, Mom?" I was curious since Mom was so frugal. I couldn't imagine her buying a TV, even if it was used.

"It was a gift," she said coldly. The look of disdain on her face was enough to tell me the conversation was over. There was no way I would ask a follow-up question, like who gave her the TV set.

I started to understand that my mom's view of men had changed since she had separated from my stepfather. Men were not liked. Men were not good people. Men were not welcome, unless they could provide money.

A couple of weeks later, Mom and Crystal were lying on Mom's bed, cuddling up and watching a TV show together. It looked like fun, so I roared into Mom's bedroom and jumped on the bed to join them.

My mother and sister immediately kicked at me to get me off the bed. I hit the floor, which was covered by a thin carpet. My knees took the brunt of the fall.

"You're a dog!" Mom scolded. "Boys are dogs, and dogs belong on the floor!"

Hearing her say that—and the way she and my sister gleefully kicked me off the bed—was one of the most crushing experiences of my childhood. My intention was to join Mom and my sister and cozy up, but they consigned me to the floor, where the dogs belong. Even worse, she and Crystal laughed at me the entire time.

I stayed on that floor for a long time, feeling like a pile of dog manure—worthless. All I wanted was love and to join in with the family.

All the emotional confidence I had gained from Mrs. Spears's speech therapy classes vaporized into thin air. *How could they kick me? Was that how they viewed me—someone who was no better than a dog?*

I was deeply hurt that day. In fact, the times when I was violated with a broomstick and beaten by my stepfather didn't compare to that crushing moment for me. The betrayal I felt from my mother and sister was tremendous, but the way it was completely unexpected hurt the most. I never would have thought that my mom and sister could treat me so shamefully.

Here's why that incident was so painful: what my mother and sister were telling me was that I didn't belong, that I really had no place to go.

But it was around this time that I found a place to belong, where Someone was already waiting for me.

8
—

BREAD CRUMBS

After being kicked off the bed by my mother and sister, thank goodness I had Mrs. Spears to make me feel special.

Besides being a great speech pathologist, Mrs. Spears was also smart. During three months of after-school lessons—an extracurricular effort she wasn't paid for—she never once proselytized. She sensed that a troubled kid needed encouragement at a significant time in his life, and she was right. The closest she came to sharing God's love was having me read stories from the Old Testament. When she had me read from Jeremiah and I learned how God knew me before He formed me in the womb, I was stunned. For a kid who had just tried to kill himself, "Before you were born I set you apart" (NLT) were the words I needed to hear.

Beyond that, Mrs. Spears never had me read from the gospels. Although she talked about God, she never shared the Four Spiritual Laws, which outline God's plan for eternal salvation. She was a public school teacher, and even back in 1974, the public school system wasn't friendly to having the Bible read during the school day in a classroom. So Mrs. Spears took a far subtler approach by asking me if I knew Moses was a stutterer and having me read engaging Bible stories from the Old Testament so I could practice forming and uttering words.

I didn't know it at the time, but every time she had me read the Bible into the reel-to-reel tape recorder, she was leaving a bread crumb for me to follow.

My best friend the summer after fifth grade was Tim Grace, a black kid in the neighborhood. We got along great and loved doing fun stuff together like riding our bikes, getting ice cream at the local convenience store, and playing sandlot baseball. I was starting to get into sports more.

Tim was a churchgoing boy, which is an understatement. My goodness. His father had passed away, and his mother took him and his brother and sister to Good Shepherd Baptist Church every time the doors were open: Monday night for a kids' Bible memorization program, Wednesday night for worship service, Friday night for youth group, and Sunday for Sunday school, the main worship service, *and* the Sunday night service. It's amazing we got to hang out as much as we did.

In fact, Tim's last name wasn't really "Grace," but everyone in the neighborhood referred to his family by that name because they were always in church and were always doing what they could to help the other people in the neighborhood. Tim's mother gained such a saintly reputation that people started calling her "Mrs. Grace," and it stuck.

One day, Tim asked me, "Would you like to go to our church's summer camp? I've gone every year, and it's a lot of fun. Can you join us?"

I'd never been to a summer camp. Up to that point, I hadn't gone anywhere except for a family trip we took to Niagara Falls.

"Uh, I don't know if we have the money," I hedged.

Tim's face brightened. "Don't worry about that! Camp's free. Listen, we'll have a blast. We'll be in the same cabin with other kids, and there are a lot of fun things to do, like swinging on a rope into the lake."

It turned out that I didn't have to sell Mom on letting me go. I imagine she looked at summer camp as a two-week vacation from having to worry about me. "Fine," she said.

My eyes took in everything as I rode the church bus with Tim to a rural area outside Cleveland. The weather-beaten cabins were rustic, but I didn't know any better. Everyone was really nice, and I liked the structure of camp: getting up each morning at a certain time, making our beds, and walking to the cafeteria for breakfast at 8:30, followed by the day's activities.

We'd always gather first in the main hall, where we sang a series of great songs that I immediately fell in love with: "Oh Happy Day," "The Blood Will Never Lose Its Power," and "Mary, Don't You Weep." My favorite, though, was the classic hymn "Amazing Grace" and its soaring melody when we sang, "When we've been there ten thousand years . . ." Sometimes when I felt goofy, I'd make a funny face at Tim each time we sang the word *grace* since that was his last name.

When we were done singing, one of the youth pastors would share a lesson from the Bible and give us a Scripture or two to memorize. Then we'd get a break to run around outside in the pine-scented air until it was time for lunch. Afternoons were spent swimming in the lake and doing crazy stuff, like jumping off a high-diving board or hanging onto a rope, swinging over the lake, and letting go.

After dinner—I loved that I could go back for as many desserts as I wanted—we met in the grand hall again to hear from Good Shepherd's pastor, Eddie Hawkins. Everyone called him "Pastor Hawk."

He was stout, he was broad, he was powerful, and he had my complexion. He told us that he was one of nine children who grew up in Arkansas during the 1940s but he'd lost both of his parents at an early age. He was quite a good amateur boxer growing up and found some success in the Golden Gloves featherweight division. Upon graduating from high school, he enlisted in the U.S. Marine Corps during the Korean War, serving three years in the military.

I was mesmerized every evening as he spoke. Dressed in a crisp blue suit, red tie, and spit-shined black shoes, he had such a great way of preaching—starting slow and building to a climax in a thundering voice. I hung on every word. I remember once he spoke about a judge sitting in a courtroom, listening to a death penalty case. The person on trial was his own son.

When it came time to render his decision, the judge had two options: guilty or not guilty. He could extend mercy and pardon his son, although the evidence was clear that he had committed the crime, or he could fulfill his responsibility to provide justice and pass the sentence—a one-way trip to Death Row.

What would the judge do? In this case, the prosecution had laid out an open-and-shut case that included the testimony of numerous eyewitnesses and forensic evidence. There was no doubt his son had committed the crime and deserved to die.

When it was time for the judge to announce the verdict, he cleared his throat. Just as he was about to speak, a man barged into the courtroom. "Your Honor!" he shouted. "I know the defendant is guilty of this crime and deserves to die, but I'm willing to pay the penalty for his actions so that he can go free."

Pastor Hawkins looked around the camp hall at the couple hundred adolescents and young kids in rapt attention. "That person who entered the courtroom is our Lord Jesus Christ. In a similar way, He came onto this earth to rescue you from your fate. Listen, we've all sinned and fallen short of the glory of God and deserve punishment. Jesus lived a perfect, blameless life, yet he went to the cross willingly and died in our place, providing a perfect sacrifice for our sins. God shows us the way to salvation. In John 3:16, it says, 'God so loved the world, that he gave his only begotten Son, that whosoever believeth in him should not perish, but have everlasting life.'"

Although simplistic, this story fascinated me. To an impressionable eleven-year-old boy, Pastor Hawk exuded an aura that said *God's way is the right way to live. Keep your nose clean. Keep your shoes polished. Show up on time, and you'll learn something.*

• • •

While Mrs. Spears introduced me to the concept of God, summer camp—the next bread crumb—gave me the opportunity to understand the Christian culture, which I had not been part of growing up. Listening to sermons deepened my understanding of who God was and why His Son came to this earth. The praising and worshiping of Jesus through rhythmic songs and boisterous singing was the emotional lift that a down-on-himself kid needed to experience.

We each left camp with a Bible. This was still a mysterious book to me and filled me with mixed emotions. I remembered one time when Big Daddy had railed against the Bible during one of our visits to see him. He thought the Bible was an evil book used by white people to dominate the poorer peoples of the world.

"It's like this, Squeeze," he told me one time. "When the white missionaries came to Africa, the Africans had the land, and the missionaries had the Bible. The missionaries asked the Africans to bow their heads and close their eyes to pray. When the prayer was done and the Africans opened their eyes and raised their heads, the Africans had the Bible and the missionaries had their land."

My grandfather also believed the Bible was used to justify the torture of Jews during the Spanish Inquisition. (Later, I would learn he had a point.) Big Daddy wasn't a fan of the Bible, and he didn't like religion of any kind because when he and Grannie had asked a pastor to perform their wedding ceremony, the clergyman responded that interracial marriage was a sin and "an abomination unto God."

Big Daddy said he didn't want anything to do with church and religion after that, but I was having a different experience. Summer camp turned out to be a great introduction to the Christian community. Everyone was so nice and loving. When I read the Bible, something stirred in my soul because God's Word spoke to me with such intimate power and truth. I believed what the Bible said: there was a reason for me being on this earth. I wasn't a mistake, but I was chosen by God for a divine purpose.

As soon as we got back home from camp, Mrs. Grace offered to take me to church on Sunday. "You can come with us. Play your cards right, and there might be lunch in it for you," she said with a wink.

Mom had no problem with me going to church with the Grace family, figuring that was better than hanging out on the streets. The next Sunday morning, I heard their car horn beep, and off I went. Good Shepherd Baptist Church was a good poke from home—around forty minutes away in East Cleveland.

The church was mostly African American. The pastor's daughter, Tina, led the red-robed choir, and man, they had you on your feet, clapping and sometimes dancing. Not only was the choir entertaining, but inspiring. Their harmony was amazing.

Pastor Hawk preached with intellect and emotion. After hearing him in the pulpit for a month or two, I noticed a pattern: he'd introduce the theme of his sermon and the main section of Scripture he would be teaching from. Then he'd amplify God's Word verse by verse, always drawing out five points, followed by a conclusion and a call to action. The ex-Marine believed in structure.

Pastor Hawk also loved using alliteration in his sermons. He'd walk through the book of Colossians talking about the power, preeminence, and peace of Jesus. He'd say that God wants three things from you—surrender, service, and supplication. He'd declare that we are to love God with our head, our heart, and our hands.

When he wasn't explaining the context of the Bible passage in his outline, Pastor Hawk was dipping into his bag of illustrations, many of which felt like they were aimed right at me. Like the time he told the story about how researchers put three frogs into a big holding tank a hundred yards wide inside a giant warehouse. The amphibians started swimming around, but then the technicians suddenly turned the lights off. The frogs had no idea where they were as they treaded water. After fifteen minutes, they got tired and drowned in the complete darkness.

The next time, technicians dumped three new frogs into the holding tank. Once again, the amphibians were swimming around when the lights got cut—except for a solitary penlight at the other end of the tank.

"Did those three frogs drown?" Pastor Hawk asked. "No—they had hope. There was a light beckoning them off in the distance. So they swam and swam and swam until they reached the other side of the tank, where there was a place for them to rest, relax, and be restored."

There was the alliteration again.

Then Pastor Hawk applied the illustration to our lives. "Right now, you may be swimming in darkness. You may be asking yourself, *Who am I? Why am I here? Why am I even on this earth?* But suddenly, you see a beacon of light off in the distance. God says, 'I know you. I've set you apart, and it's your job to find out why.' Do you know why you're here? I know. It's because you're here for a divine purpose."

I remembered what Mrs. Spears told me the last time we had met just before school let out for the summer. We were talking about Moses again, and Mrs. Spears said, "Ronaldo, look what God did with him. He helped two million people come out of darkness into the light. That's going to be you someday. I see it. I see your heart. You care, you're sensitive, and your eyes are full of love and hope. You are a gentle soul, but you are going to be strong. You have a beautiful voice. You don't hear it yet, but I believe that God is giving you a gift—a gift to speak."

"Really, Mrs. Spears?" I didn't see how that was possible. Sure, I had stuck up for Kevin Anderson when the teacher had wrongfully accused him, but that was my only experience with speaking up.

Mrs. Spears came from around her desk and put an arm around my shoulders. "Your speaking needs to be developed, but you have a gift, and God is going to use it, not just to help you but also to help your family."

"How am I going to do that?" As a kid, I couldn't fathom how this would happen.

"I'm going to tell you how it's going to work. First, you're going to start in Jerusalem."

"Where's that?" I was fuzzy on geography in the Bible.

"Don't worry about that, but that's home," she replied. "You're going to start sharing your messages, your thoughts, and what God gives you to say to your mom, your sister, and your relatives. You will see miracles happen in your home. Then you're going to go to Judea, which is the people around you, your friends. After that, God will take you to places you've never been before. That would be Samaria. You're going to have the same impact, and then God is going to take you all over the world."

This seemed incredible to me. I'd never even been on an airplane before.

"I have every confidence that you're going to travel the globe," she said.

My back straightened that day. When a teacher or an authority figure gives a child a sense of vision, a sense of hope, it's like that flicker of light those three frogs saw in the gigantic holding tank.

I had something to swim for—impacting others with my words.

• • •

I noticed something every time Mrs. Grace picked me up for church that summer—she kept the windows down so there was plenty of fresh air circulating.

Years later, she told me why. "I used to get headaches driving you to church because you didn't realize how strong you were smelling. I didn't know how to tell you that you needed deodorant because young boys don't normally need an antiperspirant at your age, but you were starting to become a young man. I got migraines that were out of this world after driving you to church!"

Poor Mrs. Grace, who was picking me up for Sunday morning and Sunday evening service, Wednesday night service, and Friday night youth group. I guess boys on the cusp of adolescence can't smell themselves.

Sixth grade is when many boys begin puberty. I was hoping to be in Mrs. Spears's class, but I was assigned to a short stump of a black woman who patrolled the classroom like a drill sergeant. She was a great teacher, but she should have been named Mrs. Napoleon for her strong presence in the classroom. Yet she was loving as well.

The best part about sixth grade was study hall. I know that kids usually don't have great memories of their study period, but I do. Study hall was in the school library right after lunch, a time when most students finished their homework or caught up on their reading.

I had a different agenda—listening to great speeches. Now that my mind had been opened and my horizons had been expanded, I was fascinated by the great speakers of my day: Martin Luther King Jr., John F. Kennedy, and Winston Churchill. I would check out reel-to-reel tapes of their most famous speeches and listen to them through headphones during study hall.

I soared to the heavens listening to Dr. King's "I Have a Dream" speech given on the National Mall in Washington, DC, two months after I was born in the summer of 1963. JFK's stirring inaugural address—"Ask not what your country can do for you, ask what you can do for your country"—gave me chills. Winston Churchill's gravel-voiced speech to the British citizenry to fight the Nazi war machine stirred my soul: "We shall go on to the end. We shall fight in France, we shall fight on the seas and oceans . . . we shall fight on the beaches, we shall fight on the landing grounds, we shall fight in the fields and in the streets, we shall fight in the hills, we shall never surrender."

Listening to their speeches over and over—as well as to other famous addresses—enthralled and challenged me. *This is possible for you, too. You can become an orator just like them. Just keep listening.*

I was amazed by the ability these great men had to speak with such fluency. My goodness, how could they put words together like that?

I brought home books about King, Kennedy, and Churchill so I could learn what made them tick. Mom, an avid reader, looked on approvingly. Whenever she took me to our local library to return and check out more books, she'd say, "There are no chains in the library. That's where all the treasure is. Everything you want to know in life is in the library."

One time she checked out a book for me about Adam Clayton Powell Jr., who had served twelve terms as a congressman representing Harlem in the US House of Representatives. He was the first person of African American descent to be elected from New York to Congress. He had died a couple of years before of prostate cancer.

"Read this," Mom said. "He did a lot for his people."

Like my mother, Powell didn't look black. His fair complexion, hazel eyes, aquiline nose, and straight black hair belied his black identity. Mom liked his looks and swashbuckling personality, and perhaps she was drawn to him since he was a well-known politician when she lived in New York City. A handsome, suave guy with a thin mustache who stood six feet, four inches tall and was known for a big, booming voice, Powell's three marriages, taste for luxury, and king-of-the-cool image made him irresistible to my mother. He was an interesting guy to read about.

I also found tapes of Powell's speeches at the school library. Listening to him as well as to Martin Luther King Jr., I learned about modulation—variation in the tone or pitch of one's voice. I listened to these men create feelings with words by saying something loudly or softly, fast or slow. I began to understand how these changes impacted their addresses. There was a lot one could do with words—like how a helicopter pilot can cause the craft to pitch and roll or go up and down. You could really create a feeling and a mood by how you said something. I began to change my modulation and listen to how that sounded.

I became consumed with reading everything out loud—and I mean *everything*. I'd walk around the house with a book in my hand, reading the text for all to hear. Naturally, I drove my mom and sister crazy, but that was the only way I could polish my diction. I'd practice turning my voice, changing the rhythm, and adjusting the cadence . . . slowing down, then speeding up. I practiced Mrs. Spears's lessons by focusing on breathing, relaxing, and overenunciating the end consonants of my words.

I checked out books from the library that had transcripts of my heroes' speeches. My favorite was Martin Luther King Jr. He had this Southern drawl that captivated me so greatly that I couldn't breathe. He was in no hurry, but he had such a way of pronouncing and enunciating his words that I was enthralled listening to him and wanted to imitate him.

I mimicked him when I read his famous "I Have a Dream" speech out loud:

Five score years ago, a great American, in whose symbolic shadow we stand today, signed the Emancipation Proclamation. This momentous decree came as a great beacon light of hope to millions of Negro slaves who had been seared in the flames of withering injustice. It came as a joyous daybreak to end the long night of their captivity.

I listened to Dr. King build a case of why, in the face of the difficulties of today and tomorrow, he still had a dream—an aspiration deeply rooted in the American dream. I did my best to channel him as I moved into the heart of the speech:

I have a dream today.

I have a dream that one day, down in Alabama, with its vicious racists, with its governor having his lips dripping with the words of interposition and nullification; one day right there in Alabama, little black boys and black girls will be able to join hands with little white boys and white girls as sisters and brothers.

I have a dream today.

I have a dream that one day every valley shall be exalted, and every hill and mountain shall be made low, the rough places will be made plain, and the crooked places will be made straight, and the glory of the Lord shall be revealed, and all flesh shall see it together.

This is our hope.

I must have read "I Have a Dream" out loud a dozen times at home, prompting Crystal to say, "I have a dream that you stop doing this."

Nothing like a sibling's encouragement, but I wasn't going to stop. When I read John F. Kennedy's speeches out loud, I imitated his Boston accent and the way he dropped the final *R*s (as in "car" becoming "cah"). I mimicked how he pronounced the letter *A* differently depending on whether it was at the end of a word ("pizza" was pronounced "pizzer") or inside of a word ("aunt" became "ahnt" and "bath" became "bahth"). I was developing an ear for accents.

This was one of my favorite passages from a speech that President Kennedy gave before the Canadian Parliament in May 1961:

> Geography has made us neighbors. History has made us friends. Economics has made us partners, and necessity has made us allies. Those whom nature has so joined together, let no man put asunder.

Like any aspiring orator, I wanted to paint pictures in the minds and hearts of people to inspire them, to motivate them, to help them see what they could not see on their own. I began to understand how public speaking was a great gift, and an even greater tool for good. To be able to walk up to a podium, armed with only words, and paint verbal pictures that stirred hearts and touched people—something that had seemed impossible just six months earlier—was within my grasp.

The more I practiced, the more I gained confidence that one day I could speak in public.

• • •

When I wasn't in school, I eagerly went to church four times a week during the fall and into the holiday season. If Mrs. Spears gave me the concepts of Christianity and the summer camp supplied me with a sense of community, sitting under the teaching of Pastor Hawk provided me with conviction. He was always pressing the congregation to make a commitment for Christ. Every Sunday, Pastor Hawk ended his sermons with a call to salvation.

"Going to church doesn't make you a Christian any more than standing in your garage makes you a car," he thundered from the pulpit. "You can be baptized so many times that the fish know you by name, but that won't make you a Christian."

Pastor Hawk looked around the audience as he let that thought sink in. "You just heard me say that the fact you're in church or have been baptized doesn't make you a Christian. So what makes you a follower of Christ? It's all about having a relationship with God through His Son, Jesus Christ. God has a destiny for you that He wants you to fulfill. He who has begun a good work in you will complete it."

And then Pastor Hawk invited those who wanted salvation to come forward to the altar, where they would meet with a prayer partner and pray to receive Christ in their hearts.

For four months, I watched a steady stream of people go forward. I was receiving a lot of preaching and teaching—I also attended Sunday school—but I wasn't quite ready to make that commitment. Mrs. Grace and other adults at the church didn't push me to go forward. They saw I was serious about God and about church, so they must have known it was only a matter of time.

On a Sunday morning in early December, while Pastor Hawkins went through his five points, I thought about how I wanted God to be my Father. As a fatherless kid, that idea was powerful to me. Then I heard Pastor Hawk say that Jesus was my protector, my teacher, my guide, my mentor, my coach, and my leader, declaring that Jesus was the one who would never leave me or forsake me.

That hit home with me. I was in desperate need of a father because the man I thought was my father had left and never come back. I had no male role model in my life.

I was lost in these deep thoughts when Pastor Hawk asked everyone to stand. He did this every Sunday during the altar call. The church was silent except for light organ music that played in the background. Probably five hundred people were in the pews.

"I would like everyone to bow their heads and close their eyes," the pastor began. "If you don't know Jesus Christ as your personal

Savior, I want to invite you to surrender your life to him today, right now, right here. It's not about ritual, it's not about religion, it's about having a relationship with the Creator of the universe."

There was the alliteration again.

"So let me ask you three questions: Number one, is what you're doing, in your flesh, really working for you?"

I'd heard Pastor Hawk ask that question many times, but on this morning, it was like I was hearing him say it for the first time. The answer, I knew deep in my heart, was no—my life was a constant struggle.

"Number two, are you tired of hurting?"

Pastor Hawk had me there. I was tired of being a hurt, emotionally bruised kid.

"Number three, do you really want a change in your life and to walk with God for the rest of eternity? If you do, the opportunity is here right now. Jesus said, 'Whosoever shall confess me before men, him will I confess also before my Father which is in heaven. But whosoever shall deny me before men, him will I also deny before my Father which is in heaven.' Right now, at this moment, if you want to confess Jesus as your personal Savior and accept his gift of salvation, I invite you to come forward and receive him."

The organ's music rose an octave. I knew I was ready. I knew this was my day. I knew this was my time.

Without hesitation, I walked down the center aisle to the front, joining perhaps a dozen others. The church was clapping. I shot a quick glance back to our row, where I saw Mrs. Grace wiping away tears.

Pastor Hawkins shook the hands of every person who came forward. "Congratulations, son," he said to me. "This is the most important decision you'll ever make."

Turning to the entire group, he said, "We're going to assign you a prayer partner who's going to lead you to the back of the church and go over the plan of salvation with you. Is that okay with everyone?"

All heads nodded.

My prayer partner, a church elder to whom I had been introduced previously, came alongside me. He was grinning and whispered his congratulations. "Follow me, young man," he said.

He led me to a room where he walked me down the "Romans Road," which teaches us that everyone has sinned (Romans 3:23), the penalty for our sin is death (Romans 6:23), Jesus Christ died for our sins (Romans 5:8), and to be forgiven for our sins, we must believe and confess that Jesus is Lord, because salvation only comes through Jesus Christ (Romans 10:8-10).

I said I understood and agreed with everything he was telling me.

"Excellent," he said. "Let me lead you through the sinner's prayer. Please repeat after me: Lord Jesus, I need you. I know that I'm a sinner. I know that I've fallen short. I know that without Jesus Christ, I will die and be apart from God. Today I want to make Jesus my Lord and Savior. I open the door of my life and receive you as my Savior and Lord. I want to become a part of the family of God. Thank you for forgiving my sins and giving me eternal life. Make me the kind of person you want me to be."

I received another Bible as a gift as well as pamphlets about living the Christian life. I was asked to attend new membership classes during the Sunday school hour so I could better understand the basics of Christianity, such as: What was my responsibility as a Christian to become a disciple? What were the sacraments of the church—taking the Lord's Supper and water baptism—all about? Why was it important to study the Word of God?

Every week, my prayer partner would call me at home and check on how I was doing—especially if I didn't go to church. But I don't remember missing too many Sunday services; I was dialed in, as they say. Plus I'd gotten into a routine with Mrs. Grace beeping her horn on Wednesday night, Friday night, and twice on Sundays.

Each time I left the house, Mom would give me a kiss and wave goodbye. She didn't have a desire to join me at Good Shepherd, but I'm sure that seeing me leave the house with a Bible in my hand gave her something to think about.

I wanted my mother to know Jesus.

Lord knows, she needed Him.

9
—

A HIGHER CALLING

After I went forward at Good Shepherd Baptist Church and asked Jesus into my heart, I started answering the phone differently at home.

"Good evening, praise the Lord," I would say with clear diction.

In those days, I never knew who would be on the receiving end of my friendly greeting—perhaps Grannie, a neighbor down the street, or the auto repair guy calling Mom to tell her that her car was fixed. If I wasn't cheerfully saying, "Praise the Lord," then I'd switch it up and say, "God bless you."

Crystal hated hearing me answer the phone that way and would race me to the living room whenever our telephone rang. She was mortified that I would say, "Praise the Lord" to a friend of hers.

"Can you stop it?" she asked. "You're embarrassing the family. Just say hi. My friends are laughing at you."

That wasn't a good enough reason to halt my new way of answering the phone. "Well, I'm a Christian now, and I want everyone who calls the house to understand that," I explained.

"Doesn't matter," my younger sister retorted. "You better stop saying 'Praise the Lord' because it's getting on my nerves!"

That wasn't going to happen, not after I got saved. My favorite day of the week became Sunday because that meant I would get to hear Pastor Hawk preach in the morning and the evening. Hearing him speak, I was like a thirsty man receiving a cup of cold water.

I remember one of Pastor Hawk's sermon illustrations, which were always unique and engaging. "The Kingdom of God is like a man crossing the middle of the Sahara desert," he began. "He's been walking for miles in hilly sand dunes when suddenly he spots an oasis in the distance. He fixes his eyes on the palm trees, and when he reaches the oasis, he finds an old man with a white beard sitting on a wooden bench. Above him a sign is affixed to one of the palms. It says, 'Here sits the wisest man in the world. You may ask him one question.'

"So the wanderer, with dust in his eyes and on his lips, steps closer to ask his solitary question. 'What is the key to happiness in life?' he asks.

"The wise old man nods, then points across the oasis. 'See the barrel of water over there? Take off the lid, look in, and you'll see the answer.'

"So the dry, dusty guy, with a parched throat, walks over to the barrel of water, followed by the wise old man. The visitor lifts the cover and naturally sees his reflection. Before he can turn around and ask the wise man, 'Is that all there is?' the old man moves like a leopard, grabs the visitor's neck with powerful hands, and instantly dunks his head into the water—and holds him underneath the surface with a vise grip.

"The wanderer's arms flail as the wise old man holds him down for thirty seconds, then sixty, and then for almost two minutes. The wanderer can no longer resist and is about to drown when the wise old man lifts his head out of the water and says, 'What do you want now?'

"And the wanderer replies, 'I just want air. I just want to breathe!' "

Pastor Hawk paused, giving us a moment to take in his dramatic story. When he resumed preaching, I knew he was about to impart an important spiritual truth.

"When your desire to know God is as strong as your desire to breathe air, then you'll know the secret to happiness."

And that's where I was in the months after I went forward for the altar call. I felt like the Lord Jesus Christ was just as important to me as my next breath of air. I could not live without Him or stop thinking about Him. When I was home, I would read my Bible before dinner and after I finished my homework. There was always something new to learn.

Meanwhile, I was also learning a lot about Christianity at the new membership classes, which lasted for eight weeks. Going to Good Shepherd four times a week, plus listening to all that great teaching, may have been like trying to drink from a fire hose, but I couldn't get enough.

In my membership class, we were supposed to come up with a personal life verse that we could call our own. I remember asking my Sunday school teacher if John 3:17—not the more well-known John 3:16—could be my choice because I liked it even more than its famous predecessor. The answer, of course, was yes, so I committed this verse to memory:

For God sent not his Son into the world to condemn the world; but that the world through him might be saved.

JOHN 3:17

When my Sunday school teacher asked me to repeat the verse word for word, I had no problem reciting John 3:17, as well as many, many other verses, because I was memorizing a lot of Scripture each week. After I gave my life to Christ, it was like my mind became a steel trap of information. I developed a photographic memory where I could recall, in great detail, information that I had seen visually on a page.

This newfound ability was the most wonderful thing: I could read a page about skyscrapers in the Childcraft encyclopedia and quote back pertinent information verbatim—like how many stories were in the world's tallest building or how many US presidents there had been. But I was spending far more time reading my Bible than thumbing through Childcraft volumes because God's Word interested me much more. I didn't find memorizing Bible verses that difficult, so I committed to memory so many verses that I lost count.

What all this memorization did was marinate my heart with God's Word at a time when I was changing in many ways during my last year of elementary school: physically, through puberty; mentally, through a photographic memory; and spiritually, through the teaching I was receiving.

I was finding out that God would be the Father I was missing in my life. God, as my Father, found a way to lead me to a deeper knowledge of Himself through the Holy Spirit. I read in the Bible that God had different names that revealed His personality traits:

El Shaddai, or God Almighty
Adonai, or Lord and Master
Jehovah Jireh, or a God who provides
Jehovah Shalom, or a God of peace
Jehovah Rohi, a shepherd and a leader

I began to understand who He was and everything He promised to be to me. What resonated most with me was how He said He was a Father to the fatherless.

Everything about my personal relationship with Jesus Christ was very real to me. You see, my newfound religion wasn't an intellectual exercise or something that made me feel better—it was all I had. I was desperate. Knowing God and His attributes became very important to me, and the more I learned about Him, the more I wanted God to be pleased with me. I knew I needed Him and could never do anything without Him—which is why I didn't want to do anything that was going to make Him leave me and take away His anointing and His favor, whatever that might be.

I understood deep down that I desperately needed God. I knew where I had come from. I knew I had tried to take my life. I knew I was mortal. But since God had become my identity and had given me purpose, I now had newfound strength to find my way in this world.

• • •

When Mom was going through her divorce, I found out that she and Dick Archer had never legally married, which threw me for a loop. Growing up, I assumed my parents were husband and wife because they told everyone they were married, but that wasn't the truth. Years later, I learned that the state of Ohio, however, had recognized their union as a common-law marriage since they had cohabited and held themselves out to the community as being husband and wife, which meant they would have to divvy up property and my stepfather would have to pay alimony. That's when Mom made it known that she wanted our house on Stockbridge Avenue.

My stepfather, who managed and owned various real estate holdings in the Cleveland area, hired a big-time downtown attorney to represent his interests since there were some assets in play.

What my stepfather didn't know was that his lawyer used to be one of Mom's "friends." I remember Mom and Aunt Ann chuckling about how they had pulled a fast one because this attorney wrote the divorce settlement in her favor. And that's why we got to stay in the house.

That was huge, but then Mom made an even bigger decision when I was eleven years old. She stopped going out alone at night, and she stopped entertaining men at our home. Instead, she got hired as a bank teller at Cleveland Trust's main office in downtown Cleveland.

From the first day, Mom excelled in her job. Customers liked her friendliness, and she got along well with everyone who came into contact with her.

One evening Mom came home and told us that the bank manager approached her with an opportunity. He said the bank was launching a new ad campaign and looking for an actual employee to feature in their newspaper advertisements. Would my mother be interested in something like that?

What I didn't know at the time was that the bank's advertising department was looking for someone just like Mom—an interracial professional woman in her late twenties. Mom was still beautiful as well.

My mom said yes, and for the next five years or so, Mom was the smiling face that graced newspaper advertisements for Cleveland Trust. I was so proud of her, and kids who saw the ads treated me with more respect. She didn't get paid a lot of money for doing this, but she received something far greater—esteem from her colleagues and the surrounding community.

Like me, Mom was finding her way.

●　　●　　●

Having a photographic memory gave me the uncanny ability to read something and then recite it backward, forward, upside down, and right-side up. I'm exaggerating, of course, but not by much. In many ways, school became easy during my junior high years.

The Cleveland public school system established junior high as encompassing the seventh, eighth, and ninth grades and high school as the tenth, eleventh, and twelfth grades. When I moved into seventh grade, my new school was Charles W. Eliot Junior High, which was a good forty-minute walk from home through decaying neighborhoods. There were no school buses in those days. I had to get up early to make the long walk with my friends. It was like a migration of the wildebeests.

Eliot Junior High was a *Lord of the Flies* kind of environment—survival of the fittest. It was rough. Eliot Junior High was a boil on the buttocks of the world. There were foolhardy and devil-may-care kids packing heat as well as gang-affiliated toughs selling drugs to their classmates. In the mid-1970s, marijuana was the drug of choice, and cocaine was starting to rear its ugly head.

When you mix a cohort of prepubescent and young juveniles in the cauldron of an inner-city school, then you're talking about a difficult, volatile environment. It was hard to learn anything except where was the best place to light up a joint during lunch. There were so many social and behavioral problems in the classroom that the harassed teachers spent most of the class hour trying to get students to sit down and be quiet.

In many ways, attending Charles W. Eliot Junior High was like being on the set of the TV sitcom *Welcome Back, Kotter,* which debuted on September 9, 1975, a week after I started seventh grade. We had our "Sweathogs"—a bunch of juvenile delinquents—in every class too.

I wasn't a Sweathog and knew that Mom wouldn't stand for unruly behavior or a lax attitude toward learning. She made sure I signed up for English, math, social studies, and science classes along with PE. At Eliot, though, I was issued textbooks with torn-out pages and sat in chipped, wobbly desks.

The well-meaning but overmatched teachers fought valiantly to maintain their sanity. If kids weren't blowing them off in the classroom by talking out loud or laying their heads on their desks and sleeping off a drug high, they were walking out of the classroom to smoke a cigarette or pass a joint among themselves, leaving behind the pungent smell of pot in the halls. Between classes, bullies picked on nerdy kids and tried crazy stunts like "swirlies"—grabbing unsuspecting teens and holding them upside down over a toilet bowl while it flushed.

I didn't participate in the pranks. I didn't smoke or drink. I didn't do drugs. I didn't want anything to do with that stuff because I had learned that smoking pot and sniffing glue destroyed brain cells. Smoking cigarettes turned your lungs black and cost you years of your life.

At this time I began taking very seriously the apostle Paul's admonition in 1 Corinthians 6:18-19 that my body was a temple of the Holy Spirit, that I did not belong to myself, that I was bought at a price, and that I was to flee from sexual immorality so as not to sin against my body.

I became aware in junior high that girls stopped having cooties and became shapely. So did all the other guys. Everyone knew who the hot girls were, and sex was a popular topic. I heard the boasting in the locker room from guys who were fooling around—or claiming to. Whether or not there was any action, I could tell that the only reason they were going to school was to meet girls and get physical.

But my thinking on the girl front could be summed up in this sentence: if you don't know Jesus, then I don't have any time for you. I didn't want to get into that nonsense. If I did talk to girls, then that happened at church. There were a couple of girls at Good Shepherd whom I liked, but nothing ever developed. I was in junior high. I knew I was too young to get involved. Besides, my main interests at the time were God and academics.

Academics, it grieves me to say, weren't important to my classmates. To them, Eliot was one big holding pen until the final stop on the schooling treadmill—the all-black John F. Kennedy High School.

I was on a different track. I *wanted* a good education. I *wanted* to go to college. I *wanted* to make something of myself because of Mom's missionary zeal about the importance of education and how it could take me places. She told me time after time how she missed out on so much learning and didn't want her children to suffer the same fate.

Speaking of places, Eliot Junior High, located in the Miles Heights area, sat on twenty acres—a huge land mass. There was so much grassland that you could run forever.

In the fall of my seventh-grade year, I tried out for the football team. I didn't have much experience playing sports. Actually, I had zero experience. I didn't have a father or an uncle who tossed a football back and forth with me, who showed me how to swing a bat, shoot a basketball, or make a layup. As for football, the only time I could remember throwing a football happened in fifth grade when I was hanging out at a nearby park and some older guys were tossing a football around. One guy, acting as the quarterback, was throwing the ball to various receivers running pass routes.

I was watching what they were doing, mesmerized by how the receivers either sped up or slowed down to run under lofty passes and catch the spiraling football in their outstretched arms. What they were doing looked like fun, but I hadn't thrown the football much before. Like I said, I had no one to coach me or help me.

"Hey, youngblood. You wanna throw the ball?"

I looked up. One of the guys saw me watching and called me over. "Sure," I said.

One of the receivers moved off to the side. "I'm going long," he said.

"Got it."

I took several steps back and watched him run in a straight line up the field. I reared back and launched the football high into the air, watching the pigskin sail for a good forty yards toward the receiver.

"Man, you have an arm!" one of the guys replied.

"I do?" I had no idea what they meant by that.

"You should become a quarterback!" he said.

So I started hanging out with these older guys—okay, they were in junior high—but they let me get some experience throwing the football. I got better and learned to calibrate how far I should throw the ball so that my receiver could run under my pass and catch it. I concentrated on my short throws when I needed to drill a shorter pass to my receiver.

I wouldn't say these guys in the neighborhood taught me a lot, but they allowed me to learn by trial and error so that by the time I started junior high, I was a fairly competent passer. When I tried out for the seventh-grade team, the coach installed me at quarterback.

Mom bought me a pair of used cleats, the cheapest she could find since she was such a bargain hunter. The cleats she found at a garage sale were so worn down that they went through the leather sole and hurt my feet. I'd practice and come home with blisters and bloody socks.

"Mom, I can't wear these cleats anymore. I'm bleeding," I said.

"But how can they be hurting you?"

Mom didn't understand what cleats were for, but then again, she had no interest in sports whatsoever. But she still supported me and wanted me to play football and other sports. She put some type of padding inside the shoes that at least made wearing them tolerable, although my feet still hurt and bled after many practices and games.

Our seventh-grade team started off with a bang—we won our first three games. Parents were calling us "Lombardi's Packers," after the legendary Green Bay Packers coach of the 1960s, Vince Lombardi. (The local NFL team, the Cleveland Browns, didn't have much of a winning tradition.) But our three wins were against other inner-city schools. The meat of our schedule would pit us against suburban schools that had much better equipment than we did—helmets and pads—and better facilities and coaching. From then on, I had to run for my life and heave the ball as far as I could down the field and hope for the best. Our opponents were bigger and faster and knew what they were doing. We didn't win another game that season.

What happened is that our porous offensive line allowed their blitzing linebackers to race through and pummel me at will. That's why I had to get rid of the ball quickly, but more often than not, once the ball left my hand, I got knocked down. Back in those days, quarterbacks weren't protected like they are today. The only time I didn't get pummeled was when I handed the ball off to one of our running backs, but most of the time I had to throw because we were behind in the score.

I played football all three years at Charles Eliot. I wasn't a great player, merely competent, but I enjoyed being with the guys and learning the game. I had fun even though I had to scramble out of the pocket to get away from opposing linemen determined to break me in two. One year, I had a contusion in my left thigh and could barely walk to class. Bruised bones and muscles were commonplace. Even though I was getting crushed, I soldiered on. My coaches liked that, and they liked that I was coachable. My goal, if I had one, was to play high school football.

When my seventh-grade football season was over, I didn't try out for the traditional winter and spring sports of basketball and baseball. Since I had determined that football was my sport, my coaches said I should wrestle and run track and field. Wrestling would prepare me for the football season because the strength training required for the sport would teach me body control and leverage. To get faster on the field, joining the track team was the way to go. I ran the 440 (one trip around the track).

When football season came around in my eighth- and ninth-grade years, I was the strongest guy on the team. I like to think that it was my German strength coming out. I could deadlift two hundred pounds in junior high.

I grew rapidly during my junior high years. I shot up from around five feet, five inches in the seventh grade to five feet, eleven inches in the ninth grade. I was medium build—not overly big, but not overly small for my age. Average. What I did have in my favor were broad shoulders, a slim waist, big thighs, and huge calves. My calves were like cantaloupes.

By my ninth-grade year, there was nothing spectacular about me except for my arm. Now I could throw the football nearly sixty yards in the air. When we got behind—which was nearly every game—my receivers would tell me, "Time to Archer it up, Archer it up." So I'd drop back seven steps and heave the ball as far as I could down the field—and hope for a miracle catch. I threw a lot of Hail Mary passes, always going for the long bomb.

● ● ●

In the springtime of my ninth-grade year, I was asked to play the role of Moses in a youth group production during the Easter season.

Moses? You mean my favorite character in the Old Testament? After Mrs. Spears's introduction, I certainly identified with the man God had chosen to lead his people out of bondage in Egypt. Three times in the story where he was called, I read that Moses had speech difficulties. I didn't know whether Moses was painfully shy and tongue-tied or was the strong, silent type who was slow to articulate his thoughts out loud, so I played Moses straight—without a stutter—just like actor Charlton Heston.

I didn't know anything about acting, but I had my dashiki ready. I memorized my lines. I threw myself into the role. My best friend, Tim Grace, played Joshua, Moses's second-in-command and the person who would take over and lead the Israelites into the Promised Land after Moses's death.

There were several scenes where I—for lack of a better word—preached to all Israel while wandering forty years in the wilderness. (In fact, in *The Message*, Deuteronomy 1:1 says, "These are the sermons Moses preached to all Israel when they were east of the Jordan River.")

"We will all fail to live as we ought to," I said while playing the role of Moses. "What we need to keep our focus on is living according to the ethical standards laid out in the Ten Commandments. God can fix your heart, if you let him."

Performing in public turned out to be no problem at all. I didn't stammer over my lines one iota. In fact, I loved being on stage and felt energized by being part of a live performance. When Moses came down from Mount Sinai with the Ten Commandments only to discover the Hebrew people worshiping a golden calf, I thundered, "Do not worship any other god, for the Lord your God is a jealous God!"

We had several performances, and each time we received a standing ovation. While the cast basked in the warm applause, Pastor Hawk bounded onto the stage, enthused by what he had witnessed. He thanked the cast and crew for all their hard work in putting on the Easter production and then took several steps my way.

"Didn't this young man do an amazing job?" he asked.

The full house—nearly a thousand people—clapped and whistled. Some shouted, "Amen!" Others clamored, "Right on, Pastor!"

I smiled and looked out at the audience. This was *fun*.

Then Pastor Hawk took several more steps toward me and placed his arm around my shoulder. "The way Ronaldo spoke Scripture with authority and articulated himself today says a lot. This young man, I believe, has a calling to preach on his life. We have to watch what God does in the future."

One of those applauding that night and beaming with pride was my mother. She wasn't going to Good Shepherd with me, but she wasn't about to miss seeing me in the lead role of Moses.

Mom was doing so well at Cleveland Trust. Her supervisors praised her work, and she got a raise. In those days, before everyone waited in a single line for an open teller, regular customers would line up at her window so they could conduct their bank business with her.

I saw how determined my mother was to prove Dick Archer wrong and keep us in the two-story house on Stockbridge Avenue after the divorce was finalized. There was no way she would lose our home because she couldn't keep the mortgage paid.

I guess my stepfather didn't know my mother that well after all.

10

—

TRANSITION

You could say that the ninth grade was a pivotal time in my life. I was in my last year of junior high at Eliot, ducking spitballs in the classroom and drugs in the hallway. Heroin was making its way into the inner city in the late 1970s.

Drug dealers targeted young men with no father, no money, and no future. What these dealers would do is give these young men money for stealing hubcaps or some other inconsequential but easy commodity to pilfer. As a reward, the dealer let them have a pinprick of heroin—just a taste of it. They'd stick a needle of heroin in the skin and release a bit of the magic elixir. On the street, the practice was called "skin-popping" because the drug was injected into the skin, not into veins or muscles.

The rush and the feeling of goodwill that came on . . . man, it was something. At least that's what I heard from one of my uncles who got hooked on drugs. He said skin-popping heroin felt like being embraced in a genuine hug, like a warm blanket being wrapped around you.

Of course, the dealers never mentioned that there was a fairly large risk of infection from a subcutaneous injection or that abscesses were the likely result of skin-popping for any extended period of time. Or that you'd wake up with a runny nose and an ache in your hip. Or that you'd experience a sudden case of the flu and bouts of vomiting. Just when you'd feel a little better, you'd realize that you'd better not be too far from a bathroom because diarrhea was coming on strong.

The reason the dealers never mentioned any of those things is because they were interested in getting you hooked—and having you pay for your next high. So you might steal a car radio and he skin-pops you one more time, and all the pain goes away. That's when you realize, *Wow, that's magical! That makes me feel better. That cures whatever's ailing me.*

Soon, and very soon, you are working for drugs by stealing stuff because it's all about the next high, the next fix. That's how these dealers built up armies of petty criminals. They got them hooked early in the inner city, including my uncles. I remember going to Grannie's house and climbing into the attic, where there were mattresses and dozens of needles and cotton balls strewn everywhere. That's where my uncles got high, and my grandmother was none the wiser.

As for me, it was a miracle of God—and I mean this sincerely—that I didn't try skin-popping or do something stupid like taking speed, known as "black beauties" on the street and Dexedrine at the pharmacy.

The reason I stayed away from drugs is because God had gotten hold of my life—and I had seen how my uncles got sick when they couldn't get their drugs. They would vomit in their beds and soil their underwear. After witnessing that stuff up close, I was scared straight.

I wanted no part of that because I believed God had a plan for my life, plus I was pretty much locked in on living the Christian life. Not only was I faithfully in church Wednesday night, Friday night, and most of Sunday, but I was reading God's Word and biblical commentaries that explained and interpreted Scripture. Pastor Hawk had told me that I could come by his office any time to borrow books from his library.

That was an offer I couldn't refuse.

One time after the Sunday morning service, Pastor Hawk invited me into his massive office. Tall bookshelves lined three walls and were filled with titles from floor to ceiling. Pastor reminded me that he enjoyed sharing his library with young, inquisitive believers such as myself.

"Here's one you might like," he said, pulling down *Spurgeon's Commentary on the Bible* by Charles H. Spurgeon. "He was an English pastor, a Baptist, who lived in the nineteenth century. They called him the prince of preachers. I think you'll find him interesting."

I sure did. Spurgeon's book had some heft physically—it was a thick book—and mentally from his penetrating thoughts and precise exposition. Within those pages were deep ideas, incredible insights, and illuminating illustrations tied to biblical texts. Reading Spurgeon is where I was introduced to theological disputes like Calvinism versus Arminianism, which attempted to explain the relationship between God's sovereignty and man's responsibility regarding salvation.

Once I finished Spurgeon's volume, I tackled other commentaries and read about the debate between Pentecostalism and Fundamentalism and learned new and very long vocabulary words: dispensationalism, eschatology, and hermeneutics. What I really ate up, though, were books dealing with prophecies found in the books of Daniel, Isaiah, and Revelation.

This being 1977, the book making a buzz was *The Late Great Planet Earth* by Hal Lindsey, which was the bestselling nonfiction book during the 1970s. I must have read and reread *The Late Great*

Planet Earth a dozen times. Lindsey cited the restoration of Israel in 1948 and the rise of what would become the European Union as harbingers that the world would end in the 1980s. I understand now—decades later—that Lindsey was wrong to speculate when the end times would start, but I was still fascinated with biblical prophecy. Keep in mind, too, that I was only fourteen years old, relatively new in my faith, and soaking up information like a sponge.

Sometimes when I was hanging out with friends at lunchtime, I'd talk about the interesting stuff I was reading as a way to engage them about Christianity. If I happened to mention that I read something by Spurgeon about God's grace, I'd get responses ranging from "Who's he?" to "That's cool" to nonverbal cues that said, *You're too much for me, man.*

And that's when classmates started calling me Rev.

"Hey, Rev, what's happening?"

"Rev, how did you do in the track meet yesterday?"

"Hey, put the cigarettes out. Rev is here."

If they did call me Rev to mock me, they never did it to my face.

I accepted their nickname as a badge of honor, especially when I went into the locker room and heard the baseball team's best hitter say, "Hey, no cussing. Rev just walked in."

The way I looked at things, if they called me Rev, that meant they knew I was sold out to Christ.

•   •   •

I mentioned that schoolwork became easy during junior high when I developed a photographic memory. Well, maybe *easy* isn't the right word, but all I had to do was look at words in a book, math equations on a blackboard, or formulas in a chemistry class handout and I could instantly recall them for days, if not weeks.

I'll never forget the time when Mom took Crystal and me to the Cleveland Museum of Natural History, which was home to millions of specimens in the fields of anthropology, archaeology, astronomy, botany, geology, and zoology. The exhibit that set off my imagination was the display of various dinosaurs inside a three-story atrium. The facsimile skeletons of the prehistoric beasts with extremely long necks—perfect for munching vegetation from the tallest trees—impressed me.

Each dinosaur stood before an anchored display sign that revealed the dinosaur's Greek- or Latin-based name, which were tongue-twisters.

Pachycephalosaurus
Albertosaurus
Tyrannosaurus rex
Brontosaurus

The display sign said that *Pachycephalosaurus* was from the Greek roots *pachy* (meaning thick), *cephale* (meaning head), and *saurus* (meaning lizard). The *Pachycephalosaurus* was a thick-headed lizard that was fifteen feet long and weighed about a thousand pounds. Its short, incredibly hard skull was framed by small horns and ended in a pointed beak.

That night, as we sat around the dinner table with Aunt Ann, I regaled my family with what I had learned at the museum, repeating the *Pachycephalosaurus* name properly along with the pertinent information regarding its height, weight, and unusual features, such as its ability to inflict some serious damage with its domed, heavy head.

My aunt nearly dropped her knife. "This is amazing," she said. "How are you able to do that?"

"Believe me, he was telling us the names of every dinosaur on the way home from the museum," Mom said.

I smiled and mentally recalled a Bible verse that seemed fitting for the occasion—John 14:26, which says the Holy Spirit will teach you all things and bring all things to your remembrance.

Mom broke into my thoughts. "And they said you weren't smart," she declared with pride.

Hearing her say that returned me to the days I was shunted off to the school basement, where I dipped my finger into water-based paint and drew houses and stick figures. I spent most of an entire school year there, learning absolutely nothing, and yet a few years later, I was a different person—mentally, physically, and spiritually.

What Mom and my aunt were seeing with their own eyes was the presence of God manifested in an ordinary child.

The way Mom boosted my self-esteem prompted another passage to come to mind, 2 Corinthians 4:7-9:

> But we have this treasure in earthen vessels, that the excellency of the power may be of God, and not of us. We are troubled on every side, yet not distressed; we are perplexed, but not in despair; persecuted, but not forsaken; cast down, but not destroyed.

At one time, I had wanted to kill myself. I was a messy clay pot. Then God turned that clay pot into a treasure chest, and seeing that happen every step of the way were the two adults who knew me best: my mom and Aunt Ann. They witnessed a metamorphosis—the power of God changing a caterpillar into a butterfly.

A few weeks later, I brought home my report card. Mom was cooking fried chicken on the stove with her apron on.

"Mom, can I show you something?"

"Of course, honey. What do you have for me?"

"My report card."

She opened the folded card and saw that I had straight As. She immediately wept tears of joy.

"That's so wonderful!" she exclaimed. "I knew you were intelligent."

I beamed from the motherly praise, but I didn't dare tell anyone at school that I got all As on my report card. No, no, no. You weren't supposed to take school and schoolwork too seriously, not in the inner city. It was a badge of honor to brag about *not* doing your homework or about arriving at school ill-prepared for a test. Those who behaved scholarly were teased for being "white" or were called names like "Uncle Tom" or "nerd." The other kids were saying, in effect, *You're not really black if you take school seriously.* I knew some kids who let their grades slip on purpose so they would fit in with their peers.

I wasn't going that route. I wanted to get an A in every class, on every test. Eventually, my friends and classmates figured out that I was one of the best students, but in fairness to them, I didn't get ridiculed, because I was a good athlete. If you were a good football player and smart, then you were cool. If you could sing in the school play and were smart, then you were cool. If you could dance and were smart, you were cool. You just couldn't be only smart. You had to have another skill.

After I brought home a report card filled with As, my mother's thinking about my future changed. I think she saw things in a new light because she was doing well at the bank and was being featured in bank advertisements. In other words, she was becoming part of the "establishment," which gave her a greater understanding of why her son could not become anything he wanted to become if she didn't do everything she could to get him out of the public school system. She wanted to give me a chance to compete for a place in college against the kids from suburban schools and private schools because she had great dreams and aspirations for me. Mom didn't see how I could get into a good college by attending JFK High, with its reputation as an inner-city, underperforming school.

"We have to get you into a better school," she said one night over dinner.

"What do you mean, Mom?"

"We have to get you out of the public schools. You've gone as far as you can go. Now we need to get you into the right learning environment."

"But where would I go?"

"I don't know. I'm still figuring that out."

Since private school was costly, especially for a single mom, Mom had a lot of thinking to do. While she was figuring out her options, a couple of cute girls flirted with me after school one day. "Let me braid your hair," one offered.

I didn't have much going on after track practice, so I said, "Sure, why not?"

I was a caramel-colored guy with curly hair, perfect for making cornrows, which were in style in the 1970s. But when I came home for dinner with a set of dreadlocks that would have made Bob Marley proud, Mom flipped out.

"That's it! You are getting out of that school! There is no way my son is walking around with braids in his hair. Are you out of your mind?"

The cornrows weren't a big deal to me; I was just messing around. And if Mom was talking about putting me into a private school, that sounded good to me. But I didn't know of any private schools in our neighborhood.

"Where would I go?" I asked.

"You know Johnny Wellsby?" she replied.

Sure, I knew Johnny. He lived a few blocks from us and was a couple of years older than me. I was aware he attended a private school because I saw him dressed in a navy blue blazer, white-collared shirt, and navy tie while he waited for the city bus in the morning.

"Yeah, I've seen Johnny around."

"He's turned into a fine gentleman ever since he started attending a Catholic school. Every time I see him, he's saying, 'Yes, ma'am, no ma'am.' Very courteous. Handsome, too. When I asked him where he was going to school, he said he was going to St. Peter Chanel High School on a scholarship. That's where you're going!"

My mind swirled. "Where's this St. Peter's school?"

"In Bedford."

Bedford? That was a good ten miles southeast of where we lived. I couldn't walk that far. Bedford sounded like another world to me, who rarely left the neighborhood. The $64,000 question was, how was Mom going to afford sending me to a private school?

As if she was reading my thoughts, she said, "I'm going to see if I can get you some kind of scholarship that will cover most of your tuition. If we can do that, then your Aunt Ann wants to help out too. We agreed that we would work overtime or get another job if that's what it takes to get you enrolled at St. Peter's."

My mom had always been an amazing provider. These days, people sometimes call it "ghetto economics," but what that meant in practical terms is that my mother would have torn off her left arm to make sure Crystal and I would not feel ashamed about our clothing in any way. Image was important to her, so she did whatever it took to make sure we had good clothing. That's why she shopped at thrift stores in affluent neighborhoods and picked through boxes of clothes at garage sales. She cooked from scratch well-balanced meals that were delicious. She was a hustler who could stretch a buck until it hurt.

As for Aunt Ann, who was single and living with us, she had a good job and wasn't marriage-minded. She, too, saw potential in me and wanted to invest in me at a time when I had only my mother to lean on emotionally, spiritually, and physically.

So the die was cast: Mom arranged the scholarships and found extra work, and I would attend St. Peter Chanel High School starting in my sophomore year. I remember telling one of my teachers at Eliot Junior High that I was enrolling at St. Peter Chanel in the fall. He shook his head, as if to say, *I pity you.*

"Just know that the As you get in this school are worth Cs in a suburban white school like St. Peter Chanel," he said.

I gulped—and wondered what I was getting into.

I would soon find out.

PART 3

TESTIMONY

11
—

BECOMING A CHANEL MAN

Talk about a culture shock.

I had never seen so many white people in one place in my life. The first day I stepped onto the campus of St. Peter Chanel High School, I actually asked myself, *Where did all these white people come from?*

Actually, I should have said, *Where did all these white* boys *come from?* Because Chanel—as everyone referred to the school—was an all-boys Catholic high school run by Marist priests. The four-year high school had a little more than one hundred students in each class and five hundred in total enrollment.

I had no idea who St. Peter Chanel was, but I quickly found out during school orientation. He was a French guy born in the early 1800s who grew up wanting to become a missionary for the Roman Catholic Church. He went to seminary and joined the Society of Mary, a religious congregation of priests founded in France and known as Marists. His wish to share the Gospel was realized when he sailed by clipper ship to the South Pacific in 1836. Life was hard on the island of Oceania, where Peter struggled to learn a new language and integrate himself with the natives. Few converted to Christianity, and when the chieftain's son asked to be baptized, the tribal leader had Father Chanel clubbed to death. Pope Pius XII canonized him as a saint in 1954.

All this Catholic stuff was Greek to me. So was the sea of white faces that surrounded me. I mean, I knew that Caucasians were the predominant race in America—anyone turning on a TV show or watching a Hollywood movie was aware that black people were relegated to supporting roles or positioned in the background—but this was the first time I had actually experienced being a minority.

You see, in my neighborhood, I was part of the *majority*. That's all I knew growing up because I didn't travel much outside Lee-Harvard. The only time I interacted with white kids was on the football field, but that was only a handful of times. My world was basically black with a few white folks sprinkled in, the principal among them Grannie.

So going to school the first day at Chanel was a mind-blowing, shocking, bolt-from-the-blue, eye-opening experience. I can't emphasize this enough: I realized then that *I was a minority*. My culture was not the mainstream culture. The way I spoke was not the mainstream language. My music—basically Motown artists like the Temptations, the Four Tops, and Marvin Gaye—was different from the Rolling Stones and the Bee Gees.

And then there was the food, which was also foreign to me. The school cafeteria served kielbasa, pierogi, and a side of sauerkraut. No fried chicken with macaroni and cheese and collard greens on the menu for me. What was served in the cafeteria reflected the tastes of the white population residing in the working-class neighborhoods surrounding Chanel, which was located in Bedford, twelve miles southeast of downtown Cleveland. Back in the late nineteenth and early twentieth centuries, waves of immigrants from Eastern European countries like Poland, Czecho-slovakia, and Hungary settled in the Bedford area, bringing along their customs as well as their Catholicism.

I'll never forget going to Mass with the student body on the first day of school. I'd never been in a high church setting—the church tower, the stained-glass arched windows, the marbled sanctuary, the baptismal font, the statues of the Virgin Mary, and the Stations of the Cross were all new to me. Candles and incense were lit by priests wearing robes and vestments, and everyone seemed to know what to do. I'd never done so much kneeling and bowing in my life.

This being the late 1970s, the Tridentine Mass in Latin was long gone, but the liturgy was replaced by a folk mass with a guy on an acoustic guitar singing "Kumbaya" and "How Many Worlds." Everyone was quiet and attentive. No one moved or swayed to the music.

I didn't mind this worship experience, but it was so different from what I knew. Back at Good Shepherd, we had organs and electric guitars going full blast and drums rocking a beat that brought people to their feet, clapping, screaming, and yelling out praise for God for twenty or thirty minutes at a time. At Chanel, the "frozen chosen" either stood like statues or kneeled on a small bench connected to the pew in front of them.

When the priest delivered his homily—the Catholic version of a sermon—midway through the Mass, he preached in a near whis-per, using a vocabulary that seemed right out of a Vatican encyclical: "To the glory and honor of Almighty God, to the Most Blessed Virgin Mary, and to the saints in heaven, may the grace and peace of God our Father and the Lord Jesus Christ be with you. As we start a new school year, let us ask the Lord for strength and renew the living springs that flow through us. We ask Him to protect us in body and spirit . . ."

Where I came from, it didn't take Pastor Hawk long to rev up his engines. "The Bible does not *contain* the Word of God;

it *is* the Word of God!" he'd thunder from the pulpit. "There is no happiness outside the will of God! If God is calling you now, don't you dare do anything else!"

In the Chanel sanctuary, no one shouted "Amen!" or "Preach it, brother!" in response to the subdued homily. Instead, we sat in stony silence as we listened to the monsignor speak in generalities about living the Christian life. I didn't look down on this approach; it was just a different way of sharing God's truth. My mindset was to take this whole new world in.

Everything about Chanel was new and fascinating to me.

• • •

I don't know what strings Mom pulled to get me into St. Peter Chanel.

She couldn't afford the sticker price for tuition, but I would imagine that the Marist fathers sized up our situation and found a price that Mom and Aunt Ann could afford. The fact that a black student *wanted* to attend a school that was 98 percent white worked in my favor in those pre-affirmative action times.

There were rules to follow. No long hair over the ears or past the collar. No facial hair. No sideburns past the middle of the ear. We had to wear clean uniforms consisting of white button-down shirts, dark ties, and dark pants. Our shoes had to shine. We had to walk straight.

In the classroom, they taught us how to sit and how to walk. "Your feet are ahead of your head. That's how a Chanel man walks," said the Marist brother teaching first period. The Marist faculty were serious about molding us into men. They showed us how to properly use a knife and fork in the cafeteria. Chanel was like a finishing school for boys.

Make that *rich* boys coming from wealthy families. I saw kids dropped off in black town cars with uniformed chauffeurs opening the doors for them. One time a student arrived by *helicopter*! As for me, I was getting up at 5 a.m. so I could catch three buses to get to school every day.

Once I set foot in the classroom, discipline was strict. Demerits, as they were called, were handed out regularly. A few too many demerits resulted in push-ups and sit-ups. A bunch of demerits meant you were washing the priests' cars. The learning environment was no-nonsense.

With all these changes, I hated my first year at Chanel. Part of it was that I came face-to-face with racism. I heard students speak under their breath, whispering things like "*Go home, jungle bunny*" or "*N—s not welcome.*" Jokes were written down on paper and put in my locker, including these beauties:

"How do you stop a black baby from crying? By wetting his lips and sticking him to a wall."
"Why are all black people so fast? The slow ones are in jail."
"Do you know why black people are so good at basketball?
It's the only sport where they can shoot, steal, and run."

All these mean, horrible jokes. Chanel was very racist when I arrived there. It wasn't a friendly place for me or the other five or so blacks on campus.

One of the other black students was Kevin Robinson, who went out for the football team with me. We were the only two blacks on the squad.

During summer practice, I wowed the head coach when he saw me throw the ball sixty yards with a flick of the wrist. "You're my quarterback," he said. Kevin, who was fast as lightning and won every sprint drill, became a wide receiver.

One warm afternoon, we were going through plays on offense. The head coach stuck his head in our huddle. "Run Post 34," he said, which was a long-pass play in which the wide receiver runs straight down the field and then cuts on a 45-degree angle toward the goalposts. My job was to put enough loft on the ball to enable an open receiver enough time to run under the ball and catch the pass in stride. Do that, and it's a touchdown every time.

"Post 34, on two!" I barked out in the huddle. "Ready . . ."

"Break!" said the remaining players, clapping in unison.

We charged up to the line of scrimmage. I looked over the defensive secondary. The safety moved to my left, where our flanker and tight end were positioned. This left Kevin Robinson with one-on-one coverage on the right side of the offensive line—a perfect situation for running a post play. Because of his raw speed, I knew Kevin would blow by the cornerback and have a good two steps on him when he made his cut to the goalposts.

"Ready, set . . . hut . . . hut!"

I accepted the hike from the center and dropped back seven steps as a pocket of protection formed around me. I glanced to my left to throw off the safety and then found Kevin on my right. As I expected, he had his defender beat by a mile.

I waited an extra second and heaved the ball up the middle of the field—where I expected Kevin to be forty yards downfield. He was wide open, and the ball arrived on time. There was nothing but green grass between him and the goal line. He reached out—and the ball slipped through his arms!

Aargh!

Kevin jogged back to the huddle with his head down. Coach was waiting for him and got in his face mask. "How much more wide open can you be?" he asked incredulously. "If that was a watermelon, I bet your black butt that you would have caught the ball!"

All time stopped. *Did he just say that racist garbage?* Kevin and I were shocked down to our cleats because Coach had used a racial stereotype to demean him.

This wasn't my first experience with racial prejudice, of course. I had watched documentaries on racism and hadn't forgotten the story of what had happened to Big Daddy on a sidewalk in Cleveland. I wasn't born yesterday. But it was still hard for me to see it so close at hand and from someone who was supposed to be leading and helping us.

As much as it hurt, I had to let the incident go. So did Kevin. We were in *their* world, and there was nothing we could do about it.

•   •   •

There were the more overt cases of racism, such as the jokes on my locker and the incident on the football field, but other instances were casual and taken for granted. For example, take my first name—Ronaldo. Back in the late 1970s, Ronaldo wasn't an American-sounding name, at least to white ears. So my Chanel teachers shortened my name to Ron, and I became "Ron Archer"—the name I go by today. (This attitude was commonplace at the time and explains why Barack Obama, two years older than me, was known as "Barry Obama" when he attended Punahou School, a private prep school in Honolulu, Hawaii.)

On the football field, my football coaches called me Ron or Ronnie, the latter as a term of endearment after I made a good play. *Way to go, Ronnie!*

I didn't experience outright racial discrimination from my teachers, but the academic rigor, as I expected, was demanding. Any reports or essays I wrote were handed back to me with instructions to rewrite. One teacher said to me, "Sorry, but you can't write well."

Taken aback, I responded, "I can write."

"No, you're writing at the public school level, but now that you're at Chanel, your writing has to improve."

So I rolled up my sleeves and rewrote those reports and essays, sometimes several times, while learning from the corrections and tips I received from my teachers. The process was exhausting because I was staying up late to do my homework and to redo work that didn't meet the academic standard, and I still had to get up early to catch my buses to school. Short on sleep, pedaling as fast as I could to make passing grades, there were times when I told Mom, "I can't compete at Chanel."

Mom never let me get too down on myself. "You're playing catch-up," she'd tell me. "You'll match them in no time, and then you're going to pass them."

I remembered what Mrs. Spears had told me a few years earlier: "Anything worth doing in life is worth doing poorly at first until you get better." I also recalled something else she said that buoyed my spirits: "Remember, what is going to set you apart is all the work you have done with your speaking."

Little did I know how speaking in public would change the arc of my high school years at Chanel. Here's what happened.

There was an incident in my American history class that escalated into a fight between two individuals. Punches were thrown, and the two students wrestled each other to the ground before being separated by the teacher and other students. The Marist father established order and then escorted them to the principal's office.

Twenty minutes later, the school principal—a monsignor—stepped into our classroom.

"Okay, who saw what happened?" he asked.

He was greeted by the sound of crickets. I looked to my left and then to my right: no one was raising a hand to speak up.

I had been an eyewitness, but could I risk addressing the monsignor? If I did, would I revert to stuttering? I rarely stumbled over my words anymore, but with everyone's eyes glued on me in a new setting at a new school, I wondered if I would freeze up. Would I be viewed as an untrustworthy snitch by these white, wealthier students that I was just getting to know and become friends with?

I decided to go for it. I felt my right arm shoot into the air.

"Monsignor, I saw what happened."

The prelate looked in my direction. "And you are—?"

"Ronaldo—Ron Archer, sir."

"Please inform me about what you witnessed, young man."

"Thank you, Monsignor. I arrived in class a few minutes before the bell with several of my classmates. Just before the bell rang, Mark Miller and Johnny Evans walked into the classroom. If I heard correctly, they were arguing about a girl they both know. I am not aware of the particulars regarding their discussion, which became heated. Mark stepped forward in a threatening manner, and when he did, I saw Johnny throw the first punch. The glancing blow set off a melee between them, which was broken up by Father Griffin and other students. And that is where we find ourselves at this moment."

The monsignor's mouth opened up in amazement. "Well, thank you, son. You said that well."

The following day, I received a message while sitting in my homeroom, a short classroom session in which a teacher recorded attendance and students listened to a news show produced by the administration and read by other students. The message was short and to the point: *Please report to the principal's office immediately.*

My heart shot up into my throat. *What have I done now?* I wasn't sure, but it sounded like trouble.

I walked into the monsignor's office expecting the worst— which would be the loss of my scholarship for some malfeasance. Maybe I had spoken out of line. I didn't know what I had done. I was still finding my way in a white world.

"Take a seat, Master Ron," the monsignor said as I entered his office. I accepted a chair in front of a massive cherry wood desk.

"My goodness, you are articulate," he began. "Who taught you how to speak so well?"

I breathed a heavy sigh of relief. "Well, I was a stutterer for a long time, but I worked very hard at improving my diction and elocution.

I don't stutter anymore, although there are occasions when I slip up if I'm upset or angry. I owe all of my progress to a sixth-grade teacher named Mrs. Spears. She took an interest in me at a time in my life when I didn't think anyone cared if I lived or died."

"That's wonderful to hear, young man. You speak with such a beautiful cadence, and I know you know what that word means. Your voice is almost *harmonic*."

I sat a little straighter in my seat. Getting called into the principal's office was turning out to be a good thing.

"Ron, if it's okay with you, I want to put you on our news show, starting tomorrow morning. We need someone with a distinctive voice to anchor our program. And we will pay you something for your troubles. How does fifteen dollars a week sound?"

I thought the monsignor's generous offer was incredible, if not unbelievable. I'd have to rake leaves all day in the neighborhood to earn that kind of money.

"That sounds wonderful!" I exclaimed.

"Excellent, but please know that you need to arrive at school a half hour early to review the script and practice. Then you will broadcast live from our media department precisely at 8:15, the start of the school day. Broadcasts generally run five minutes. You still think you're up to the challenge?"

"Yes, I would love to try something like this."

Basically, what I was asked to do was read a script that contained relevant news about St. Peter Chanel High School at the beginning of the school day before students dispersed to other classes.

I'd never read anything out loud for others to listen to, but there was always a first time. The homogenized scripts were generally straightforward, bland news reports of past sporting games and announcements of future events, things like:

Last Friday, the Chanel High basketball team defeated number six-ranked Benedictine 49-44, which improves the

Firebirds' chances of qualifying for the state championships later this month. Tim Gallagher was the leading scorer for Chanel, pouring in twenty-one points to improve the Firebirds' record to 13-7.

Besides the latest sports news, there were announcements about class events, upcoming school plays, career day, the Red Cross blood drive, and teacher-parent conferences.

The monsignor and the media department loved my work, and the following year, we switched over from a closed-circuit intercom system to television. Now I addressed my fellow students through a live remote that aired on TV screens hanging in every classroom. Looking into a camera while reading the news was a good learning experience.

I blossomed as a "news anchor," and my grades really picked up; my report card my junior year contained nothing but As. Mom was right: it was only a matter of time until I caught up to my peers and held my own. On the gridiron, I won the job of starting quarterback that fall, which carried a lot of responsibility. I was doing my part to change the view of African Americans at a nearly all-white school, and that felt good.

My center was another junior, whom I'll call Bill. Quarterbacks and centers develop a close relationship because the QB starts each play by putting his hands directly underneath the center's rear end to accept the hike of the football. I also felt a kinship with Bill because his older brother, John, had been part of the production crew for the morning news and announcements during my sophomore year. John had been a huge help to me before he graduated.

After football practice one day, we were getting undressed when Bill had a question for me.

"Do you think you could see if the TV crew needs another writer? I'd like to give it a try," Bill said.

I had no idea if Bill could write well, but it didn't matter. "Sure, I'd love to help you out," I said. "Your brother was a big help to me, so it's the least I can do."

Bill smiled. "That would be great. You're a good n—!"

Did I just hear right?

Bill saw the shocked look on my face and immediately back-pedaled. "I don't mean that in a bad way at all. Gosh, I think I said the wrong thing."

"That's okay," I mumbled.

There was an awkward silence.

"Do you know how I was raised?" he asked.

"No. Of course not," I replied.

"Here's the deal," he said. "When I was growing up, whenever one of my parents went grocery shopping, they would always make sure they wiped off the food—fruits, vegetables, packaged goods—as soon as they got home. They said we had to do that in case black people had touched it.

"The second thing they did was to teach me that we came from outer space and black people were already on Earth as monkeys, but we came here to civilize you. That is why we had slavery. Slavery was used as a way to civilize the missing link between man and monkeys. That was you all, so I believed that. As a matter of fact, I thought you guys had tails when I was growing up. I believed that until I took my first shower in junior high, when I didn't see any tails on the black kids. I know it sounds crazy, but that is what I was taught."

I was aghast. *People really believed this racist stuff—and taught it to their kids?* It blew my mind. I was wondering what to say when Bill picked up where he left off.

"You know what, Ron? You've changed my view of black people. Everything I have learned about black people from my parents is not true. You're a great guy. I also know you're smarter than me. You're a leader and go out of your way to help people. In fact, you're more of a Christian than I am. Because of you, I view black people differently now."

My mind raced back to what Mrs. Spears said one time: "God will take you to places you've never been before. That would be Samaria."

I had just had my first Samaritan moment. I had impacted someone from a different background, a different race, and a different culture.

And that felt good.

●   ●   ●

At the end of my junior year, I was called into the principal's office again.

Once again, the monsignor had a smile on his face. Actually, his smile was a little sneaky.

"You know what?" he said, as if he were thinking out loud. "We need to shake things up around here. We need to change the culture of the school, and I know just the person to do it."

Then he looked at me with a sly grin.

"Me?"

"Yes, you."

"What do you want me to do?"

"Ron, St. Peter Chanel has established a tremendous legacy since we opened our doors nearly twenty-five years ago. We have sensational alumni, and we have a substantial endowment, but we've never had a person of color lead the school. I would like you to consider running for the position of student body president. Being president is a prestigious position. If elected, you'll be involved with the trustees, you'll go to country clubs, you'll be part of writing policy, you'll be on the judiciary committee, and you'll be on the finance committee—all great experiences to list on your college applications.

"Normally, the title of school president is reserved for the legacies. I want to change that. If you become our next student body president, you'll have to do a lot of work, but you'll get your own office, you'll have access to our staff, you'll get a stipend, you'll get a Chanel blazer, and your picture goes up on the wall. Becoming student body president is a highly visible position."

I was excited by the prospect but doubtful it would happen. "Sir, have you looked around?" I asked. "How am I supposed to get elected student body president? You can count the number of blacks in this school on two hands."

"I'm aware of that. But I've watched you. The white kids here love you. They follow you. You are our quarterback, a leader. Your grades are excellent. You know the Bible as well as a seminary student. I know that you can make a difference."

"Can I sleep on it?" I wanted to pray and ask the Lord for direction.

"Sure you can, young man."

That night, I flipped open my Bible to the book of Jeremiah, the first chapter—the place where Mrs. Spears had me first read. Two verses jumped out to me:

> Be not afraid of their faces: for I am with thee to deliver thee, saith the Lord. Then the Lord put forth his hand, and touched my mouth. And the Lord said unto me, Behold, I have put my words in thy mouth.
>
> JEREMIAH 1:8-9

The Lord will put his words in my mouth.
That's all I needed.

The next day, I told the principal he could count me in.

The election campaign could have been ripped out of the pages of a Hollywood screenplay. The premise: fatherless black student tries to get elected president of an all-white Catholic high school but runs into roadblocks. Add in the differences in social class and a dash of youthful testosterone, and you had the makings of a spirited, contentious election pitting blue blood "legacies" with generational suffixes like III and IV after their names against an "upstart" black senior with no family history at Chanel, no influence in the Catholic community, and no money behind his name. The fact of the matter was that I was a nobody—an inner-city kid with no connections, no father, nobody on the booster club, and nobody on the finance committee competing against wealthy classmates whose last names adorned buildings at the school.

I heard the buzz around school when I announced my candidacy: *No monkey's going to sit on the student council.* But I also knew there were plenty of open-minded and godly young men willing to hear me out and get beyond race.

I put up flyers around the school and prepared for a debate that would be televised on the school's closed-circuit system. Then I walked around school introducing myself to sophomores and juniors who didn't know me. I made sure I touched base with the students in my class.

For the televised debate, I felt like I had an edge. As the school's news broadcaster, I was used to working the camera, which raised my comfort level. I knew that I wanted to talk about my faith during my closing argument:

> My fellow students, I grew up attending an inner-city school in my neighborhood—the Lee-Harvard area of Cleveland. I still live there. So I know what it means to grow up in the inner city, which is why I can assure you that I know how special it is to attend St. Peter Chanel.
>
> Back in fifth grade, I was a stutterer who was scared to raise his hand in class. Then a teacher named Mrs. Spears volunteered to work with me. Not only was she a great speech pathologist, but she also introduced me to the Bible, which set me on the road to learning about who Jesus was.

When I was in sixth grade, I asked Him to come into my heart as Lord and Savior.

My faith in Christ opened the door for me to come to Chanel. My faith has brought me this far, and now I am seeking to become your leader. I believe that you earn your way by serving others. Together, we are going to make this school great and leave a legacy that no other class has done. We are going to raise money, we are going to go out into the community, we are going to help the poor, and we are going to make a difference. You will be proud to be part of this great school. That is why I humbly ask for your vote tomorrow.

The following day, against a field of four candidates, I received 75 percent of the votes to win the position of student body president of a prestigious country club school. The other students did not see race, they did not see class, they did not see color—they saw a servant leader. Even though I was a minority, even though I wasn't one of them, they elected me student body president because of my experience and how I spoke to them. The racist students that wanted me out of there my first year chose me to be their leader.

Winning the election changed my life forever. I saw the world differently and learned that if you bring your best and share from your heart who you are and don't back down, people will give you a chance.

I learned two lessons that day: 1) Things that seem impossible with men are possible with God, and 2) If God is for you, who can be against you?

At that moment, my family took notice. At that moment, God became even more real to me. A Scripture that spoke to me at that time was Matthew 5:16: "Let your light so shine before men, that they may see your good works, and glorify your Father which is in heaven."

That became my theme: *Let them see.*

Looking back, I can say that my election sparked a revolution in my life and in those closest to me—my mother, my sister, my aunts, and my uncles.

Because they were watching me very closely.

12

—

FROM A SERVICE STATION TO A CHURCH SERVICE

One of the best things about my senior year—besides being student body president—was driving my own car to school. Mom had a friend who wanted to get rid of a rusty, well-traveled 1970 Chevy Impala station wagon for dirt cheap, so the opportunity to avoid getting up at the crack of dawn and riding three municipal buses to Chanel each morning greatly appealed to me.

I was happy to cut my commute to school by more than half. Sure, my beater stood out among the shiny Mustangs and BMW 2002 coupes in the school parking lot, but I didn't care. These were the wheels I could afford. Best of all, no one put me down for having a crummy car. I believe it's because I was viewed on campus as a leader, and people respected me. *He's a poor kid, but he's hustling. He's going to be somebody.*

I think I paid $200 for the Chevy station wagon from money I had saved up from a part-time job at a Standard Oil of Ohio gas station in Shaker Heights, an idyllic, leafy suburb with a reputation as one of the wealthiest communities in the country. I was a "grease monkey"—the guy who pumped your gas, checked the air in your tires, checked all your fluids (engine oil, radiator coolant, and windshield wiper fluid), and collected your money when you drove up to the full-service pump. I usually worked one or two week-nights after classes and football practice and picked up a longer shift on Saturdays.

I'll never forget the time a bejeweled woman in her mink coat drove up to the full-service pump in her classic Studebaker.

She rolled down her window on a cold, gray, windswept after-noon. "Fill it with leaded premium, young man," she said.

"Yes, ma'am," I replied.

The cultured woman looked to be in her fifties. I doubted her gloved hands had ever touched a gas nozzle in her life. Her Stude-baker ran on leaded gasoline, and we were one of the few stations still offering leaded gas in 1980, which was being phased out by the EPA at the time.

"You might have some trouble finding the gas tank," she said. "It's under the trunk."

I'd never filled up a Studebaker before. Sure enough, I had to get on my knees and reach under the trunk to insert the nozzle into the gas tank. I clenched the handle, and leaded gas flowed into her tank.

It looked like I didn't have the nozzle in right, so I adjusted it—and the hose popped out and sprayed leaded gas on my face and into my eyes.

It felt like a hundred million needles had been stuck in my eyes simultaneously.

I rolled around on the ground, yelping in pain. The station manager saw the commotion and came running to my aid. He rushed me to the service bay, where he prepared an eyewash solution. My entire world was blurry, and my eyes felt like they were blistering. I had never experienced such sharp pain before in my life.

Eventually, the soothing eyewash acted as a salve, and the pain dissipated. When my eyesight returned, I breathed a sigh of relief— and whispered a prayer of thanks. I took a week off work to heal and visited an ophthalmologist. After his examination, he said, "You're lucky that your eyes were not permanently damaged. I think you're going to be fine. I predict that you'll make a full recovery."

When I returned to work, I found my manager to give him the good news—and an apology. "I'm sorry I wasted all that gas. Here's ten dollars to cover the cost of the gas that spilled out," I said in a contrite tone.

My manager looked at me like I had a screw loose. "Are you serious?" he asked.

"Actually, I am. I'm a Christian, and I wasted ten dollars of your gas. I want to pay it back."

The manager clasped my hands in his. "You keep your money. But your offer impresses me. Listen, as long as you need a job, you'll have a job here for life."

That was nice of him to say, but working as a grease monkey taught me that this was the kind of job I *didn't* want for the rest of my life.

I think that's why Mom got me the part-time job in the first place. Sure, working as a gas station attendant taught me responsibility, allowed me to have my own car, and gave me some spending money, but I learned something far greater while working at the gas station: making a career out of performing hard, manual labor for low pay was not what I wanted to do after I graduated from high school.

They say a picture is worth a thousand words, and I sure got a picture of what it was like to don olive-green overalls and crawl in mud and slush to change a tire or perform simple repairs. But the biggest impression I received at the gas station came from toiling alongside an older black gentleman named Bubba, who had spent all his working life as a grease monkey. He was only forty years old, but he had a gray beard, yellow teeth, bloodshot eyes, busted knuckles, and arthritic hands that bothered him when cold winds whipped off Lake Erie. He was a hardworking man with a wife and two kids, trying to take care of his family.

"I didn't take advantage of school," he told me one afternoon while we waited for customers to drive up to our gas pumps. "I didn't study or get good grades, so this is what I have to do now. Don't make my mistake, young man. Without an education, this is what you'll be doing for the rest of your life."

I felt like I had received an oracle straight from the heavens.

Bubba wasn't finished. "We're proud of what you're doing in that white school, being president and all that," he said. "Keep it up. Keep getting good grades. You'll be glad you did. When you stop working here, we don't want to see you again."

I worked five to fifteen hours a week at the Sohio gas station for a good year. Not only did I learn lessons about life, but I also learned how to change tires and put new ones on old rims. That skill came in handy with keeping my Chevy Impala in running condition. When my tires got bald, I couldn't afford a new set, so I did what my mother would have done: I mounted old tires that I took off people's cars when they got new tires at the station. These old tires still had a bit of tread left, so to me, they were still good. I'd wear them down until the steel belts showed through.

I needed to keep my Impala repaired and on the road since I used my station wagon to take people to church on Sundays. I had a little route that I followed, picking up folks from different parts of the community. I got teased about being the youngest driver ever for a "church van" as well as for piloting a car with a saucer-sized hole in the floorboard on the passenger side's front seat. Look down, and you could see the pavement pass by.

The toughest part about driving was getting a driver's license. I needed my birth certificate, but when Mom presented it to me, she had an embarrassed look.

"Take a look," she said.

My official name was Ronaldo Isaac Turner.

Turner?

"Where did that name come from?"

"Long story."

"I'm listening."

"When I had you at the hospital, I knew I couldn't afford to pay, so I used a phony name on the birth certificate."

This was unbelievable. Knowing my mom, she pulled the name out of thin air. "Didn't anyone ask you for ID?" I said.

"In those days, nobody asked you for ID. You were who you said you were."

"So what happened when you left the hospital?"

"I snuck out a back entrance when no one was looking and got a ride home with my brother Michael," she replied.

Having my last name as *Turner* on my birth certificate even though I was enrolled in school as *Archer* created some problems at the local DMV. Actually, "problems" is understating things by a long shot. Straightening things out turned out to be a major headache with the state bureaucrats.

"Yes, ma'am. I understand that my birth certificate says that my last name is Turner. But my mom made that name up. And I know my mother's driver's license says she is Elizabeth Peru. Let me see if I can explain that. You see, she never married Dick Archer, who I thought was my father when I started school, but he really wasn't my father. Mom had me use his name anyway, but now they're divorced even though they never married. Yes, I know it's all very confusing . . ."

The embarrassing and complicated exercise reminded me of why I hated my last name growing up. In my adolescent mind, I took on the name of a man who abused me, who resented my presence, and who went out of his way to reject me. This created feelings of abandonment. I became bitter wearing the name of a man who didn't protect me and brutally beat my mother within an inch of her life.

When I heard all the talk of "legacies" at St. Peter Chanel, I realized I didn't have one. I didn't come from an intact family with two parents. I didn't know who my real father was. My mother came from a broken family and brought that dysfunction into our family life. For me, the past was a huge question mark, an abyss.

This is why when God said *I am your Father*, hearing those words meant so much to me. Those weren't empty words. I needed a father. I needed a heritage. I needed a legacy. I needed something to grab onto that was real for me.

With God as my Father and the Holy Spirit as my Comforter, I was going to be okay. Becoming part of the family of God was attractive to me at a time when I really needed it. Sure, I was becoming articulate in my speech and thought of myself as a somewhat handsome student-athlete. My life may have looked good on the surface, but I still had all this garbage underneath some very murky water. I had to drain my own swamp.

Uppermost in my mind was the fact that I was wearing the name of a man who didn't want me as his son. But then I read in Exodus that Moses—my favorite character in the Bible—received his name not from his Hebrew parents but from Pharaoh's daughter, who found him as a baby in a papyrus basket among the reeds on the Nile River.

I came to understand that God gave Moses his name for a reason, and He gave me the name "Ron Archer" for a reason as well. I decided I was going to accept what happened and make Archer into a great name, if that would be the Lord's will.

• • •

Notwithstanding the way she lived her personal life, my mother did instill in me traits such as discipline, integrity, and character. For instance, I saw her working herself to the bone to keep me enrolled at Chanel, where I was on a partial scholarship. To earn extra money, she moonlighted by cleaning offices and bathrooms in a high-rise building located in an upscale district near downtown Cleveland. After leaving the bank at 4:00 p.m., she joined a janitorial crew and swept floors, cleaned out ashtrays, dumped trash cans, and cleaned restrooms from 4:30 to 7:30 p.m., five nights a week, to set aside money for my schooling.

I know that cleaning toilets—and guys' urinals—wasn't a job she relished. Sometimes after school, when it wasn't football season or I wasn't working at the Sohio gas station, I would help her out to support her and to help her finish early.

Cleaning office buildings was an interesting experience—and humbling. Many times, people were still working at their desks or cubicles when we arrived, and they would either look down on me or look at me like I wasn't there. The vibe I picked up was *If you don't have a degree, then that is what you have to do.*

Back then, smoking was still legal in a work environment, and I had guys who flicked ashes into their ashtray and nodded their heads for me to empty them. *That's your job, pal.*

Then I'd clean toilets only to have guys working late dirty everything up again, which meant I had to clean the urinals and toilets all over again. Like I said, it was humbling to be the student body president at a well-respected private school and the captain of the football team and to have some white-collar guy look down on me.

My respect for what Mom was doing to keep me at Chanel rose even higher. After putting in a full day with the bank, she cleaned offices without complaint. Like I said, she kept her eyes fixed on the long-term goal—getting me a solid, well-rounded education that would take me places in life.

I vowed not to waste this opportunity.

• • •

Midway through my junior year, after football season was over, I dropped by Pastor Hawkins's office to check out more Bible commentaries from his expansive library. I liked reading the observations and teachings of well-respected biblical scholars after I was done with my homework.

Pastor Hawk, as you can imagine, had taken an interest in the high school kid with a ravenous appetite to learn everything he could about God, His Son Jesus Christ, and what it meant to lead a Spirit-filled life. One afternoon, when I returned a couple of books, the pastor motioned for me to sit down.

"Ronaldo, the elders were talking to me about lightening my load around here, starting with the Sunday evening service. Ever since I saw you take on the role of Moses in the Easter play, I've felt that God has an anointing on your life to preach. I'd like you to take Sunday nights for me. They're all yours."

Talk about an unexpected offer! I was so excited that I feared I'd stammer back a response, so I gave myself a few extra moments to collect my thoughts.

"Pastor, what an honor. I won't disappoint you."

"I know you won't."

Looking back through the years, it's crazy to think that a fatherless sixteen-year-old would be asked to preach from the pulpit of a church with more than five hundred members, but that's what happened. I took this charge as seriously as I had taken anything in my life. I knew I had to pray about what God wanted me to share. I knew I had to study. I knew I had to write and rewrite my sermons. I knew I didn't want to approach the pulpit without knowing exactly what I wanted to say.

It would be presumptuous to declare that I took to preaching like a fish takes to water, but speaking in church sure felt natural. From the first minute I stood in front of the congregation, I *loved* sharing

God's Word and inspiring others to turn away from sin and renew their lives.

Like Pastor Hawk, I usually incorporated an altar call at the end of my sermons. Each time I issued the invitation, we had ten, fifteen people coming forward. Word got around that sensational things were happening at Good Shepherd on Sunday nights. Within several months, the evening church service exploded in attendance. All week long, I counted the hours until I would be in the pulpit again.

I could always count on Crystal being there on Sunday nights. Just as Tim Grace was my best friend, Tim's sister, Robin, was Crystal's. Six months or so after I started going to church with the Grace family, Crystal joined us.

Crystal was drawn to church and to God for all the right reasons, and she loved the social aspect. Popular with her peers, Crystal was quite the social butterfly, a bubbly Miss Personality who was also a dancer. Sometimes she felt I was too religious and told me I talked too much about Jesus, which embarrassed her. She said I never smiled, never laughed, and was too serious about life in general and about school in particular. Maybe Crystal was right, but I was a sober young man who didn't have a whole lot of extra time to hang out with friends.

Crystal would tell me, "I've never heard anyone preach like you, but at the same time, you're cramping my style. I mean, I love you, you're great, but I'm different than you, so don't expect me to be like you. And don't come around being Jesus to everybody and expecting me to do the same. I want to have fun. I want to relax. I want to be normal. You're raising the bar too high for me and all my friends, which makes me uncomfortable. You're way too serious."

I'll say this: Crystal always spoke her mind. I knew where she stood. But I also gave her some slack because she had made a profession of faith about a year after I did, so I knew she was a work in progress, just as we all were.

As for my mother, I knew she wasn't saved yet. You'd think she'd want to check out Good Shepherd since her kids were spending so much time there, but she never did, except to see me in the Christmas play. After I started preaching Sunday nights, she'd run into well-meaning folks at the bank or grocery store who'd tell her, "You really need to hear your son preach . . . he's the next Billy Graham . . . he's a breathtaking speaker." Even my sister sang my praises to her. "My goodness, Mom, Skeezix is a different person in the pulpit. You should hear him preach. You wouldn't recognize him."

And yet still Mom stayed away.

One Sunday, I made arrangements to meet her and Crystal for lunch after the Sunday-morning service and Sunday school. I loved Mom and wanted to acknowledge the special contribution she had made in our lives.

I can't remember what we talked about that afternoon, but I certainly didn't tell her that I planned to preach that evening on the grace and mercy of God by telling the story of Rahab, the "harlot of Jericho," who protected two Israelite spies who sneaked into the fortified city to get the lay of the land. Rahab told the spies that the citizens of Jericho had been scared to death of the Israelites ever since God parted the Red Sea and then swallowed up the Egyptian army.

Nor did I share with Mom about how, in my research, I learned that Rahab indulged in "venal wantonness" by opening her abode to local men and traveling merchants looking for more than just a room for the night. Rahab prostituted herself, just as my mother had done at one time. For Mom, it was a matter of survival. For Rahab, Scripture is not clear *why* she entertained men in this way, only that she did.

After an enjoyable lunch, we went home. I excused myself and said I needed to go over my notes and do some last-minute sermon prep. And then I drove myself to Good Shepherd since I liked to arrive early and get ready to preach.

The way they do things at Good Shepherd, and at many black churches, is that the preacher sits in an oversized chair onstage—

known as a chancel—and looks toward the congregation during announcements, presentations, etc. When the choir is singing and the band is playing during worship, he stands.

That evening, I noticed that the church was around half-full, meaning there were about 250 people in attendance. I was rocking a bit with the powerful music when I saw the most amazing sight: Crystal and my mother were entering the back of the church! I was overwhelmed with happiness. We didn't make eye contact as they looked for a place to sit. They entered a pew toward the rear of the sanctuary.

And then I remembered: I was preaching on Rahab the prostitute. How would my mother react?

When it came time to deliver my sermon, I shot up a quick prayer and approached the pulpit. I was seventeen years old, in my senior year of high school.

I set my notes on the pulpit and stepped away. When I preached, I liked to move about to keep my audience engaged. I also modulated my voice to draw their interest. I wanted them to listen to me closely, so I let my voice rise and fall to emphasize a particular idea.

"Here is this woman Rahab, who was not Jewish," I began in a slow warm-up. "She was not part of the royal lineage. She was not perfect. And yet God chose her because of her faith."

And then I made my first point. "Here's the thing. God chooses not to use perfect people. God uses imperfect people to reach other imperfect people, to bring them to a perfect God, which in the end is a perfect work."

I described how God doesn't use the shiny and the clean and the perfect. "There are rough folks in the Bible," I said. "I call them 'God's gangsters.' David was rough. He killed one of his best friends and took his wife. Abraham was a loathsome coward who basically pimped his wife, Sarah, saying, 'She's not my wife, she's my sister. Go ahead and take her.' Jacob was a con man. Moses was a murderer with a criminal record. Look at the disciples. Peter was a rough fisherman who denied knowing Christ three times. There was Doubting Thomas. You have all these characters in the Bible who weren't shining examples of virtue. And yet God, in His mercy and grace, took them and poured Himself into them and used them to do good in spite of their imperfections."

I paused to let the congregation have a moment to gather their thoughts. Then I dove right back in.

"God does not call the qualified. He qualifies those He calls. We should say, 'Yes, Lord. I know I'm not perfect, but here I am. I'm not qualified, but here I am. My pedigree is not the best, but here I am. I have fallen, but Lord, here I am. Take me as I am and use me for your glory.'"

"And this woman named Rahab hid two Israelite spies, knowing that if she was caught, she would be killed. She believed that the army of Jericho would be no match for the Israelites. As for the way she lived her life, Rahab was not perfect, but she was trying her best to do God's will. She made a deal with them and said, 'When you come back, don't forget my kindness to you. I saved your lives, and in exchange, I ask that you spare my life and the lives of my family.' She made this request even though there is no sign in Scripture that her family was living with her. The spies told her to tie a crimson cord to her window, and that would be a sign to the Israelites to spare her and her family."

I paused again, and a thought came to mind: *That was what Mom did. Her whole life she was thinking about her family.* "How do I help my brothers and sisters? My children? How do I help them?"

"This woman Rahab was not royalty, was not educated, was not anything special, but because of her faith and saying yes to God, she became the great-great-great-great-great-great-great-grandmother of Jesus. This woman was brought into the royal line of Christ. This woman became part of the genealogy of David and Jesus. Only God can do that," I said.

I stepped off the stage and paced in front of the congregation. Before I offer an invitation to become a Christian, I want to get down to the people's level. When I explain the way to salvation, I want to show everyone that I'm part of them, that I am with them, and that I'm going to help them. I always walk on the floor like a cross—across the front, as in a horizontal crossbeam—and then up the aisle, mimicking a vertical beam.

This was the moment to change the timbre of my voice to a softer tone. I needed to become gentle. I knew what was needed—not judgment, not bravado, just a quiet, soft, loving explanation of the mercy and grace of God.

"He can change your legacy. He can change your future. He can change your family. He can change your path. And look what He did. That was it for Rahab. She bought into that. I believe God is doing that and has done that and keeps doing that. And that is what it's all about, yes, it is."

This was an occasion where I *wanted* to issue the invitation. I walked several rows up in the first aisle. With my right hand holding the microphone and left arm extended, I asked everybody to stand.

"Now I'd like you to bow your heads while I ask you three questions," I said. They were the same three questions that Pastor Hawk always used when he invited people to ask Jesus into their lives and receive eternal life with him. I had learned from the best.

"Is what you're doing working for you?" I asked.

"Are you tired of hurting?"

I took my time.

"And do you want to see a remarkable change in your life?"

I looked around at the sea of bowed heads while I moved more to the front of the congregation. "Do you want to accept Christ as your personal Savior? If so, just raise your hand."

I couldn't help myself. My eyes searched for Mom in the back. And then I saw her—and her right arm was raised!

My heart skipped a beat, but I knew I had to stay focused. A dozen other hands shot up into the air.

"What I want you to do is repeat the sinner's prayer after me: 'Lord, I know that I am a sinner. I know that I fall short. I know that all have sinned and come short of the glory of God. None are righteous, not one. But if I confess with my mouth the Lord Jesus and believe in my heart that God has raised You from the dead, I will be saved.'"

I told everyone they could open their eyes. "If you have done that from your heart, you have been saved. You are now a Christian, but that is just the beginning. The second step is becoming a disciple, where you now step out of your past life and into a new life. This is where you join with other Christians who can disciple you to become a follower of Jesus. And if what you said is truly real, then you can demonstrate it by stepping forward and coming down here to the front to say, 'I want to join the body of believers. I want to learn how to live as a Christian. I want my life to reflect this inward conversion, and I need help to do that.' I urge you to take this step. Remember, Jesus said if you deny him before men, he will deny you before our Father in Heaven, but if you publicly acknowledge him before others, he will also acknowledge you before our Father in Heaven."

And then I saw the most wondrous sight—my mom was working her way out of the pew to come forward. Crystal was right behind her in a show of support. Mrs. Grace, who was in that row, was wiping away tears.

Moisture formed in my eyes as well. As Mom made her way down the aisle, along with the others who were making a public demonstration of their faith, applause erupted inside the sanctuary—and in Heaven.

Mom could barely walk from all the tears she had shed. She came to me, and I wrapped her in a bear hug.

"You did it, Mom," I whispered into her ear. "You really did it."

• • •

Mom and I had a moment, for sure.

After our emotional embrace, an older woman led Mom to a room behind the sanctuary, where she was prayed for and given a Bible as a gift, as well as important information on what it means to live the Christian life.

Mom started attending membership classes right away, where she was taught the core concepts about Christianity. After six weeks, she was ready to get baptized.

So picture the scene.

Good Shepherd Baptist had a baptismal pool behind the pulpit and behind and above the choir risers. A staircase led to the baptismal pool, which was really a big tub. The way they did things at Good Shepherd, men and women donned white robes over their outer garments and were led to the baptismal pool, where one of the pastors or church elders performed the baptism.

There was never any doubt who was going to baptize my mother—her son. Whereas Mom's decision to come to church when I was in the pulpit and then respond to my altar call was something that just happened, her baptism was a joyous, planned event that we both looked forward to.

She looked radiant in her white robe as she demurely approached the baptismal pool. I helped her step into the waist-high water and then joined her in the pool.

I took a deep breath and looked out to the congregation. Perhaps only Pastor Hawkins and the Grace family knew the journey Mom had been on. None of that mattered because we all come to the Cross for the same reason—we are sinners. All pretenses and past history are stripped away.

That Sunday morning, I placed my left hand on the small of my mother's back and looked into her shimmering eyes.

"You are one of the greatest women I know," I began. "The journey you have been on, doing whatever it took to raise a family like you did, the strength that you showed, the intelligence you displayed, and the love you shared is something I will never forget. But now you know there is an even better way to live, and that way is with Jesus. I am honored that God chose you to produce a son who would be used to help you come to a saving knowledge of Jesus Christ. My life was saved so that your life could be saved. The full circle is that the seed in your womb was the very fruit you would eat to know Jesus."

I paused and let those thoughts sink in, and then I raised my right arm to the heavens.

"Mom, do you accept Jesus Christ as your personal Savior?"

"Yes, I do."

"Do you want to renounce and die to your old life and walk in newness of life in Christ?"

"Yes, I do."

"Based upon your confession of faith in Jesus Christ, I now baptize you in the name of the Father, the Son, and the Holy Spirit."

I lowered Mom into the water and lifted her back up.

She felt as light as a feather.

EPILOGUE

In the early 1990s, I was in my late twenties when I launched my own company, which I called Archer & Associates. We specialized in teaching the corporate world how to implement self-directed work teams and transformational servant leadership.

This was the career I was building after I graduated high school, where I was the first black student body president. I then attended college at Baldwin Wallace University in nearby Berea, Ohio, and graduated with a B.A. in Communications and a minor in Theology, all the while working for two major companies—the Eaton Corporation and the Ross Corporation. In the midst of this challenging but exciting time, I preached on Sundays and was installed as a senior pastor at the First Baptist Church in Berea.

While I was director of corporate training at the Ross Corporation, I started lecturing on the side, speaking at various symposiums and seminars. As my speaking dance card filled up, I believed the time was right to start my own consulting firm. Doing so, however, was a leap of faith since I would be on my own.

Well, not completely on my own. My first two hires at Archer & Associates were my mother and my sister, Crystal. If there was any way I could provide good, steady, and well-paying jobs for them, then I wanted to do whatever I could to make that happen. This was something I'd dreamed of since I was a young boy, especially after watching Mom work herself to the bone to keep us clothed and fed and take on extra work to keep me in school at St. Peter Chanel.

Another reason I wanted to hire Mom was that she had been shaken up when a bank robber approached her teller window, pointed a pistol at her, and demanded all the money in her drawer. She complied and nothing further happened, but let's just say that Mom wasn't looking forward to showing up for work at Cleveland Trust every morning.

As for Crystal, we had matured and become a loving brother and sister. We both understood the providence of God in our lives and that everything we had gone through was part of His divine will that could make us better or bitter. We chose to be better.

When I started with Eaton and had some money coming in, I helped out with Crystal's college bills. After she graduated from Cleveland State University, she came to work for me and earned her master's degree in organizational behavior at Case Western Reserve University in Cleveland. I made her my account executive in charge of managing relationships, interpreting the data, and writing all the reports.

I wasn't sure if I could afford to hire my mother and sister when I asked them to join my new company, but I trusted the direction God was taking me. Mom was thrilled, especially when I sweetened the deal with a fancy title: Vice President of Whatever You Want to Be. Her duties included performing all the small but essential tasks that freed me up to do what God had gifted me to do—speaking and consulting.

One evening at Archer & Associates, I was working late, sitting in the conference room and reviewing a batch of marketing materials. I had leased office space on the top floor of a sixteen-story, glass-covered building in Independence, Ohio, ten miles due south of downtown Cleveland. A blanket of twinkling lights stretched out to the horizon.

Mom was still in her office even though it was getting close to eight o'clock. She walked into the conference room and sat down next to me.

"I'm so proud of how you negotiated your first million-dollar contract with SC Johnson Wax, son. You are an amazing human being to me, what you've been able to accomplish by yourself."

I was touched. I rarely saw Mom's tender side. I was about to say something, but she continued, "I just want to let you know that I'm sorry."

"Oh, Mom, that's okay." I wasn't sure what Mom was referring to, but it really didn't matter.

"No, listen to me," she said. "I'm sorry I wasn't able to hug you more. Show you more emotion, show you more support."

"That's okay, Mom. Really."

"No, I need you to understand that it's hard to give what you don't have. It's hard to give what you never got. I wanted you to be strong. I didn't want to baby you or spoil you. I now realize that was a mistake. I see now that boys need to be kissed and hugged and shown affection, just like girls. But I didn't know that when I was raising you."

"Mom, if you had known better, you would have done better."

"Yeah, but just let me say this to you. I know a lot happened to you. But a lot happened to me. I'm not going to get into everything. What I can tell you, son, is you just don't know what people will do to you when they know you have no place to go. I was the oldest when all hell broke loose in our family. Mama was sick. Daddy was away. I was the oldest, and I didn't know what was up or down. Throughout this time, there was no one to *protect me*—no one to protect me at all."

Tears welled up in my mother's eyes as I thought back to my early twenties when Mom's sisters and brothers filled in the gaps of her early years. I knew that Mom had a lot of professional male friends who helped her in exchange for her company after abusive Dick Archer left.

What I didn't know is that my mother had been sharing herself with patrons since she was a teenager.

It had all started when Mom was sixteen. Her father was in prison. Her mother had survived a scary bout with cancer but was left disfigured and blind in one eye. They had lost their home. Back in those days, welfare didn't exist. The Great Society was still a few years off, so Grannie and seven children were on their own. They made do as best they could, but they were isolated—like they were marooned on their own island. The family discovered what extreme poverty was all about.

There were a few times when my mother and her siblings came home from school at lunchtime—a common practice in those days—but there was nothing in the house to eat. Aunt Ann told me she has never forgotten sitting in a chair at the dining table, swinging her legs back and forth to take her mind off her growling stomach. After thirty minutes, she and her brothers and sisters walked back to school, so hungry they could barely concentrate on their afternoon schoolwork. Her brothers had shoes with holes in their leather soles. Her mother needed medicine but couldn't afford it. Their electricity had been turned off.

"Son, I had to do what I had to do," she continued. "I'm not proud of it, but it was either live or die, and I chose to live. I tried some things in New York, but it didn't work out. I just wanted to make a better life for all of us. Sometimes beauty in the wrong place and circumstance can be a curse and not a blessing. I was a sheep among wolves, and many times, the wolves won."

Tears were streaming down Mom's cheeks, but she wasn't done yet.

"I had dreams, too," she said. "I had great dreams. I loved school. I wanted to basically live the life you're getting to live. But life changes when everyone is depending on you. That said, I just want to tell you that I'm sorry for what happened. I thank God for you every day."

My eyes glistened, and I reached out to take my mother's hands. "It's okay, Mom. Really."

My mother had lost so much while growing up. My heart broke for her. There was no judgment. Rather, my heart was filled with love for my mother who had given me so much, including a chance to live.

She was just sixteen when I was conceived. My biological father had not been killed in Vietnam, as she had once told me; he was one of her customers. And the pimp who controlled my mother's affairs told her there was no time for a baby—so she tried to abort me back in the days before abortion was legal. No matter what they tried by way of home remedies, the pregnancy continued, which left only one option—a back-alley, coat-hanger abortion. Someone laid her on a table and attempted this grisly procedure, but again, that baby would not die.

That baby was me. Those abortion attempts caused some of the physical problems that resulted in me being so sickly as a child.

But now, years later, I felt nothing but compassion and forgiveness for my mother, who had been put in an impossible situation. She had done her best with the tools she had.

Mom leaned forward. "You know that Christmas song 'Mary, Did You Know?'" she asked. "That song reminds me of you and me. I didn't know I was raising a man of God who would preach God's Word on Sundays. I didn't know what you would become or that God had plans for you to save me."

Mom began to sob, and I wrapped an arm around her and held her close. "I love you," I whispered.

I had never seen my mom that vulnerable, that weak, that human. I realized she was not just my mom; she was also a woman who had really never been loved or protected, never coached or mentored, never encouraged or nurtured. She'd had to survive by her wits and her guile and her beauty.

And now all these years later, we found ourselves in my company's conference room, sitting at a long table, both of us in tears, understanding and acknowledging the grace and mercy of God.

That's when we went to a whole new level of closeness, trust, forgiveness, and understanding. Psalm 30:5 came to mind then: "Weeping may last through the night, but joy comes with the morning" (NLT).

*　　*　　*

For many years, although I was speaking around the world and sharing how people can turn pain into power, scars into stars, stumbling blocks into stepping stones, failure into fortune, tragedy into triumph, and misery into ministry through the saving power of Jesus Christ, I was afraid to tell my own story.

I kept it under wraps for a lot of reasons. It was dark, it was difficult, and it was hard to face the past because the aftermath of my turbulent childhood never left me. How could I ever forget what had happened to me? Even today I have to focus on elocution to avoid stuttering. Even today I can hear the voice of my stepfather and have to rely on God daily to remind me who I am.

After I turned fifty, though, I learned the power the Lord had given me, not in spite of, but *because of* my story. I was meeting with the vice president of a bank as part of my executive coaching business. He was a great leader, but he was struggling to keep his life together. Alcohol was his salve.

When I met with him, I noticed he wasn't engaged. Nothing I said had any impact, so I probed a bit further.

"What's bothering you?" I asked. "Is there something you're holding back?"

Suddenly, feelings that had been dammed up for decades sprang forth. "I was molested and raped as a young boy," he said. "No one knows. Not even my wife."

When I heard this, I felt a huge tug in my heart. That day, I shared my story with him—the one you've just read and the one I had been afraid to share. It was dark, it was difficult, and it was hard to face the past, but I saw an immediate change come over him. There was hope in his eyes that said *I'm not alone. Someone else knows what I went through.*

I was surprised that my story had caused the breakthrough for him, but I shouldn't have been. My own breakthrough came through reading the stories of Moses and Jeremiah. What gave me hope when I was hopeless was knowing I wasn't alone. And Scripture says that believers overcome the devil "by the blood of the Lamb" and "by their testimony" (Revelation 12:11, NLT).

After this meeting with the bank vice president, I knew I had a duty and a responsibility to share my story publicly. I decided to grip it and rip it at the International Gideons Convention held in Philadelphia during the summer of 2014. At this convention on Friday, July 25, 2014, I didn't hold anything back in the eight-minute window I was given to speak.

Perhaps you've seen my testimony on YouTube. To date, more than nine million people have watched it, a number that boggles my mind. Because I was given such a short time to speak, I had to condense many details that evening. Now you've read the full story.

Sure, I had a rough upbringing, but from where I stand today, I can say it's all good—and that's because I have Jesus Christ in my life. Thanks to His grace and mercy, I am not caught in a cycle of regret and bitterness. Through His redeeming work, He has changed my pain into power and my tragedy into triumph. And he can do the same for you.

Mine is a story about what belief can do, and I'd like to leave you with four "believe" statements that I hope will help you as you consider your own story:

Believe God is greater than your pain or predicament. I have never forgotten the abuse, the name-calling, or the loathing of classmates when I was a stuttering mess. My childhood was traumatic, but I also realize that my experiences are not unique. Many people have similar tales of the abuse they endured. You may be one of them, broken by emotional or physical pain from the past.

As sure as a morning sunrise, we all experience pain in life, yet God promises that there is purpose in the pain. I would not be who I am today—in terms of character, resolve, and insight about the human condition—if my childhood had been different. I've learned so much about myself and others through my travails, and I can say with confidence that God's light shines brighter in my story because of the darkness I've endured.

My advice to you is to walk the path that God has set before you, knowing that He loves you and uses your hurt and pain to bring Him glory. Everything you've gone through is a down payment on your destiny. Let me encourage you with the reminder that "the LORD is close to the brokenhearted; he rescues those whose spirits are crushed" (Psalm 34:18, NLT). "He heals the brokenhearted and bandages their wounds" (Psalm 147:3, NLT). "He will wipe every tear from [your] eyes" (Revelation 21:4, NLT).

Don't let the pain of your past or fear of the future keep you from God's appointed presence in your life right now.

Believe that failure is not final. We are all massive failures at one time or another, but God has always been the God of the second chance who prefers to mend rather than discard. Adam and Eve messed up in the Garden. Abraham was a liar. Jacob was a deceiver. Moses was a murderer. David was an adulterer. Paul was a blasphemer. Yet God used all of them in a mighty way, even after their failures.

Perhaps you still feel the pang of regret for opportunities missed and mistakes made. If you've stumbled and fallen and are feeling unworthy to be close to God because of your actions, Jesus is still waiting for you with an outstretched hand and a message that failure is not final. Let him help you turn tragedy into triumph and imbue you with confidence to move forward.

Believe that God has a purpose for you. When Mrs. Spears asked me to read "I knew you before I formed you in your mother's womb" from Jeremiah 1:5 (NLT), those words transformed my life—and they can revolutionize yours as well. God has a particular purpose for you. You aren't here by some biological happenstance or a metaphysical accident. God knew you before you were created, and He planted you in the right family at the right time for the right purpose. You are part of God's plan for the universe, and He has something He wants you to do. Ask for God's guidance as you seek to discover His purpose for you.

Believe that God is ready to use you where you are today. The apostle Paul writes, "We are God's masterpiece. He has created us anew in Christ Jesus, so we can do the good things he planned for us long ago" (Ephesians 2:10, NLT). You are unique. You are a Picasso, a Rembrandt, a Mozart, a Raphael, an Einstein: there's no one in the universe like you. When God breathed life into your nostrils, He made you a living soul with a divine purpose, and He's ready to use you today.

Don't let the deceiver tell you that you're not good enough. God knows the worst things about you yet still loves you. He knows all your sins, all your faults, all your foibles, all your errors, and all your evil ways, yet by His grace and mercy, He would die for you again. That love should give you great joy as well as an understanding that God is with you to the end of the age and that everything works together for your good and His divine purposes (see Matthew 28:20; Romans 8:28).

So let me leave you with this point: God does not call the qualified. Instead, he qualifies those who call upon Him.

Call on Him today.

ABOUT THE AUTHORS

RON ARCHER is an author, business executive, NFL chaplain speaker, and leadership trainer for corporations and the military. Born prematurely to a seventeen-year-old single mother in the ghetto of Cleveland, Ohio, Archer had a severe learning disability and stuttering disorder when he was young. He experienced a radical spiritual transformation, which helped him rediscover his voice. In 1984, Archer was awarded the Martin Luther King Jr. Leadership Award from Alpha Phi Alpha fraternity (Dr. King's fraternity) for becoming the second black student body president at Baldwin Wallace, leading leadership classes, being president of the local Fellowship of Christian Athletes (FCA), and lead counselor for the local Upward Bound program, leading revivals and Bible studies for the students and the community on the college campus. Since then, he has traveled the globe inspiring millions with his testimony. In 2014, a video of his life story went viral and has been watched by more than nine million people. He has traveled extensively throughout South America and Central America and neighboring Caribbean islands, reaching more than 250,000 people a year through his speaking engagements.

MIKE YORKEY is the author, co-author, or collaborator of more than one hundred books, including *The Shot Caller* with Casey Diaz and the bestselling *Every Man's Battle* series. He and his family currently reside in California.